The King of the Jews

The King of the Jews

28 Moments with the Son of God

BEN PUGH

RESOURCE *Publications* · Eugene, Oregon

THE KING OF THE JEWS
28 Moments with the Son of God

Resource Publications
An Imprint of Wipf and Stock Publishers
199 W. 8th Ave., Suite 3
Eugene, OR 97401

www.wipfandstock.com

ISBN 13: 978-1-62564-497-8

Manufactured in the U.S.A.

To the members of Eagles' Nest Church, Nottingham,
and the staff and students of Cliff College,
who allowed me to test out much of this material
with them in sermons.

Contents

Preface

This book had its origins in the blogosphere as a series of posts on *Dr Ben's Devotional*. However, it also has a pre-history that is traceable to a very early passion for the idea of climbing inside the world of the Bible. This passion probably had its origin around the time that I heard the great David Kossof for the first time, when he came to speak at Millmead Baptist Church, Guildford, UK. I was an art student living with a Christian couple and they took me along. I also read his book, *Bible Stories,* which was one of the only books I owned other than the Bible itself and a *Crudens* concordance. Being a good Jew, his skill was mostly with the Old Testament.

Don Francisco is not a name you hear mentioned a lot these days but I will never forget the impact of his songs back in the late '80s. His Southern accent which, as he sang, was super-imposed on the likes of Peter and John, only seemed to bring out all the more authentically the rural, rustic simplicity of the biblical fishermen of "backwards Galilee." One of the most evocative lines was, "Me and Andrew, we'd been fishin' best part of last night. We'd caught nothin' for all our tryin', come the dawn of the day."[1]

Not long after my first encounters with Don came another Southerner: Rick Renner. In 1992 he came to our church and left a lasting impact on everyone. He was a rather unusual preacher. He came from Tulsa but was not of the usual Word of Faith crowd. This guy had done a degree in Greek and specialized in expounding New Testament passages word-by-word from the Greek. He would extrapolate messages from the etymology and usage of each and every

1. Francisco, "Come and Follow Me," *He's Alive.*

Greek word, and with great drama. He seemed to have a slightly unsavory delight in describing the various methods of torture and slaughter employed during the Neronian persecution but, at least as far as the New Testament letters were concerned, he really set the scene for me. He did for the letters what Don had done for the Gospels.

Partly inspired by him, I went on to learn Greek myself, and also acquired a massive library consisting of various other volumes of ancient literature as well as biblical and theological dictionaries and commentaries: anything that I thought might help me to inhabit the world of the New Testament and one day be able to invite others into it too, like Don and Rick had done. This scholarly phase brought me to a cul-de-sac of very dry study that seemed to make me no better at inhabiting Bible Land than I was before, and even worse at inviting others into it. By now I was being allowed to develop my teaching gift in a fifteen minute slot in a home group. I can remember the night when, thinking I had developed some really excellent material that gave the sophistic background to First Corinthians chapter One, I found myself speaking of this to four awake but glassy-eyed people interspersed with three that had crossed, not into the world of the Bible, but into some other more dream-like state. Nearly half my audience was ostensibly unconscious after only five minutes about the sophists of Paul's day. My bringing-the-Bible-to-life project was dead.

Not until I came across the work of Jim Bishop much more recently did the whole project spring back to life again. He applied the fruits of good New Testament research in a creative, journalistic—you might even say embellished—way. In fact, Jim was doing just what David, Don and Rick had done. In his *The Day Christ Died* he was writing embellished Gospel narrative. In my preaching I had already begun to go that way. I had, by this time, been regularly speaking in a church that had a significant number of people with little or no Christian collateral knowledge of the Bible and it had taken years of adjustment and re-adjustment to find a method of preaching that they could engage with. Simply telling the story of the six trials of Jesus, or of a collection of resurrection appearances, all in a vivid and embellished way seemed to be achieving some success. Jim now helped me to do this. Before long, I felt the need to develop this kind of material, not only for my various speaking engagements, but also in written form. There was soon a process going on in which my sermons would become blog posts and my blog posts would become sermons. And now, the content of that blog series has been further enlarged and adapted into what you have in front of you. And all thanks to David, Don, Rick and Jim.

This book can be used either on your own or in small group and is designed to last exactly a month. The chapters do vary in length but none would take an average reader more than four minutes to read, and each chapter tends to conclude with a reference to the biblical passage that the chapter describes, and a suggested prayer. Sometimes there is more than this, sometimes less.

I hope you enjoy reading this as much as I enjoyed writing it.

ONE

Five Defining Moments

The cross of Jesus can too easily become an object of veneration in its own right. The line of the hymn, "simply to thy cross I cling" can sometimes be to the whitening of the knuckles. Yet Paul preached "Jesus Christ and him crucified." Let us ponder, therefore, some moments that define for us who it was that died on that cross and rose again. These, I hope, will give us a three dimensional Jesus.

My selection of the foregoing five events is not incontestable and, if the truth be known, the need to find exactly five chapters rather than some other number was dictated by the structure of this book as a 28-Day devotional. The other sections already fell naturally into a six, a seven and a ten. What I have chosen are five events from the first year of Christ's ministry that were definitive of all that was to come during his second and third years.

Here we see the emergence of King Jesus and the inauguration of his kingdom on earth. These are, in many respects, heady days: a first flush of glorious ministry in Galilee.

The Temptation

The day at Jordan being baptized by John had left Jesus with much to ponder. He had known for some time that he had come from God. His daily conversations with the Father made all this very clear. Yet, somehow, the voice from heaven declaring, for the benefit of everyone present, "You are my beloved son, in whom I am well pleased," had brought home the extent to which his calling was not like that of anyone else who was ever to live. The "well pleased" part was a reference to one of Israel's most cherished prophecies about a coming Messiah-King, a coming Deliverer, a longed-for Savior of the nation.

He went into the wilderness prompted by the presence of the Spirit who had come upon him at baptism and had now begun to guide him, acting as Adviser to the King. The Adviser bade him go, not to the Temple Mount or the Fortress of Antonia to proclaim himself King, but into the barren moonscapes of the Judean desert. The nights were cold though the mornings were beautiful as the haze began to lift over the rounded formations of weathered rock and the sky turned pink. The days were mercilessly hot and his skin turned dark brown. Hunger pangs eventually subsided and fellowship with the Father was close and warm. Many new insights were given him that made him ready for the coming three years' of teaching.

After a few weeks of this, Jesus began to notice how thin his arms had become and how much harder it was now to stay warm at night. Soon, the close fellowship seemed to slip from his fingers and a growing sense of foreboding began to replace it. Then the hunger pangs returned. These were quite unlike any hunger he had felt before. It was painful and induced a sense that he was dying out there with no strength left to get to the nearest village to buy bread. He sat as the sun set one evening, wondering whether he would see another morning. He stared at a pile of rocks of a kind that were common in those parts. They were known for their close resemblance to loaves of bread. He woke very early the next morning to the same sight, and the same gnawing pangs.

An evil presence gathered about him. A thought entered, "Why don't you command them to become bread? You're the Son of God. Why die of hunger? Use your authority and tell them to become bread." Moses in the wilderness received the manna from God. If Jesus was to be the prophet that Moses predicted would come, then maybe providing bread for the people was part of that mission. And it starts here in the wilderness, just like Moses in the wilderness. Here was his time to practice miraculous bread provision. But, using the force of Scripture: "Man shall not live by bread alone but by every word that proceeds from the mouth of God," he saw off the evil presence and its appealing suggestion. The Kingdom he was about to begin would result in an Israel within Israel, a truly spiritual repository of people who would then be a light to the nations, not a gaggle of gluttons begging for bread and following for food. And besides, where his own needs were concerned, he would rather trust God, the same God that sent him into this situation.

Somehow, he now found himself on the pinnacle of the temple. The sky was turning pink, and a gold strip was shimmering on the horizon. In the courtyard below, priests in white, who all looked grey in the early light, were igniting the morning sacrifice. "Throw yourself off," said a dark and sinister figure next to him. The rabbis had long predicted that when the Messiah came he would descend into the midst of the temple courts, there to proclaim himself king. Further suggestions entered his mind. If he was the Son of God, such things are not a terror but an opportunity. Maybe God himself was trying to say: "No. Don't be afraid. Just as Moses had the staff that turned into a terrifying snake and then back into a staff again, so now with this. Confront the terror of falling through empty space but await the miracle of supernatural rescue. And as with Moses and the people of Israel, this will be your sign. You could perform this feat again and again and even your cynical family members will believe who you are and listen to your message." This had been the main concern as he received insight after insight, teaching after teaching, and parable after parable out here in the wilderness: "who will listen to me? They all know me. Even John the Baptist knows me from childhood." But a light greater than the light of Lucifer was within him. That light brought to his mind the passage: "You shall not tempt the Lord your God." Of course: it was clear now. Whatever his faith in his Father meant, it could not mean the presumption of throwing himself off a cliff as a public spectacle.

Farrar quotes the nineteenth century philosopher James Martineau at this point: "An action is wrong which, in the presence of a higher principle, follows a lower; an action is right which, in the presence of a lower principle, follows a higher." This highlights to us that Christ's temptation was, as the Greek word suggests, more of a "test" than a "temptation." He was not being tempted to follow evil rather than good: to murder rather than not murder, to steal rather than not steal. It was more subtle than that—as are all the most important tests that you and I will ever face. It was a test about two goods, neither one morally evil, but one better than the other in the light of his mission from God. Would he choose obedience or expedience? Would he submit to his Father or choose a shortcut? Would he grasp the goal or treasure the process, think only of ends or be mindful of means?

Next, the devil is arrayed in the garb of a king, an emperor, with a laurel wreath around his head. Rather less subtle now. He has shape-shifted into the likeness of one with the world at his feet, like Caesar himself. Smiling but silent, the figure stretches out his hand to slowly gesture towards a panoramic view of all the kingdoms of the world. If Christ had power over all of this he would be the king of kings without a struggle. There would be no pain, only glory. The mission that his Father had sent him on, and which the Spirit was now upon him to fulfill, would be accomplished in an instant as the bequest of the imperial figure standing next to him. He turns back to the smiling figure who then speaks: "Bow down and worship me." Enigmatic, he stares at Jesus as though envious of him: an odd jealousy for someone professing to own everything.

Though the force of the temptation was strong, yet it was clear that the mask was now off and that Jesus was being asked to do something overtly wrong. "It is written: 'You shall worship the Lord your God and him only you shall serve.'" Jesus is now very faint, but angels appear and strengthen him with food.

Text: Matthew 4:1–11

Prayer: Lord, it's not the summit, it's the climb, it's not the goals, it's the game, it's not the destination, it's the journey, it's not the end that justifies the means, but the means that justify the end. Please help me to keep choosing the right way to get to where I want to be. Amen.

The Manifesto

To say that the ministry of Jesus got off to a slow start would be an understatement. After the temptation, we find the emaciated Jesus back at the Jordan, only now a little further upstream where John had gone to continue his ministry. There he acquires his very first followers (Peter, James, John, Andrew, Philip and Nathanael) and these not as a result of any magnetism of his own, it seems, but because he was pointed out twice by John: "Behold, the Lamb of God! There he is!" Once they got to spend time with him, that's when it became clear that they had "found the Messiah."

From the Jordan, they make their way North to Galilee, where all of them were from. There they attend a wedding in Cana: the famous water-into-wine incident. Passover looms and soon they make their way South again to Jerusalem. This is Jesus' chance to try to introduce himself to the religious authorities. Despite the controversial cleansing of the temple incident, they take little notice of him. Only the common people were interested in his message.

So, after the Feast of Unleavened Bread, he takes his small band of helpers into the Judean countryside to assist the work of John the Baptist. He allows his disciples to do some baptizing. These leads to rumors that he is starting up a rival ministry to John's. The Baptist's ministry was supposed to prepare the way for his and it was perhaps confusing to see Christ himself helping with it.

He withdraws from there and begins to journey back to Galilee where, so long as familiarity with the boy Jesus did not breed contempt, receptivity was always going to be greater. Galileans were much more cosmopolitan open-minded people, not like the insular Judeans. They passed through Samaria to find, in the people of the town of Sychar, their very first real success in about three months of travelling and ministering together. Sadly, they could not risk staying there for long since hanging out with the despised Samaritans for too long could jeopardize their ministry to the Jews. So they press on.

It seems their fortunes begin to turn. They arrive in Cana, where Nathanael was from and where news of the water turned into wine had spread. News reaches them there that the son of one of Herod's courtiers was dying. With a mere word, he is healed. The power of the Spirit was very obviously upon Jesus and the Galileans open their synagogues to him. Everyone is charmed by his preaching. He is a breath of fresh air. It is now time to lay out his stall, to state in unmistakable terms what he has been up to. To do this, he chooses his home town of Nazareth.

Everyone is hastening through the sunny streets of Nazareth this June Sabbath day. It was customary to hurry to the synagogue, showing eagerness for God's Word, and to saunter idly home again as though pondering the Scriptures and sorrowful that the service is now over. This service was to end rather differently to that. All the synagogues had been eager to hear him and this one was no different. The Law had been read and explained, and now it was the turn of Jesus to read a portion from the prophets. We do not know whether this was from a lectionary as later records would indicate, since Luke's account is itself, the earliest record we have of first century synagogue life. It is likely that, at this stage, services were highly flexible and adaptable. Jesus reads an adapted version of Isaiah 61:1-2, with a line removed (about healing the broken hearted), a line added (from Isa.58:6 about setting the oppressed free) and cut off in mid flow so that the stanza is made to finish on "the year of the Lord's favor," and not finish with ". . . and the day of vengeance of our God." The net result is to emphasize that God's Year of Jubilee had come in which people would be released from all the things they had got themselves caught in. The news was addressed, in the power of the Spirit, to the "poor." The poor were those described in the passage as adapted by Luke's Jesus: the captives, the oppressed, those so caught in sin that they were blinded by it. God's favor would turn their fortunes. Then he added: "Today, this Scripture is fulfilled in your hearing." The atmosphere was electric. All the rabbis would quote other rabbis and discuss the finer exegetical points. Jesus, on his own authority, says, "This is it." Allowing that to sink in, he illustrates to his audience just how broad this appeal is. It could include Syrians like Naaman, or widows from near Tyre and Sidon. It is an appeal to anyone who fits Isaiah's description. Suddenly, these open-minded Galileans become about as closed as you can get. Somehow, he walks away from the attempted lynching that follows. Time to move on to Capernaum.

Text: Luke 4:16–30

Prayer: Lord, seeing such a great offer rejected makes me want it all the more. I'm poor Lord. I need your freedom. I need to be released from the deceptive and seductive power of sin. I've tried everything and have come to believe that you alone can work your miracle in me. Set me free Lord Jesus. Amen.

An Amazing 24 Hours

It became necessary for Jesus, and possibly his family as well, to move away from Nazareth. The fishing town of Capernaum on the shores of the beautiful Sea of Galilee, home to his four closest followers, was a good choice.

This Sabbath began in the same way as that fateful Sabbath in Nazareth. Jesus made his way to the synagogue. The sound of Christ's footfall mingled with all the others that trod those black asphalt streets between black dwellings to the gleaming white marble of the newly built synagogue: the center of the town's social, spiritual and educational life.

Jesus had already become something of a local celebrity though few had so far recognized him that morning, his face obscured as it was by his headdress. Reports were still circulating not only of the things he had done in Jerusalem at Passover, but also the miraculous healings and authoritative teaching that had already graced his return to Galilee. Everywhere, his message had been similar: "The time is fulfilled; the kingdom of God is at hand. Repent and believe the good news." This message he readily teased out of a number of celebrated Old Testament prophecies and expounded them in novel and spellbinding ways in synagogue services in the towns of Galilee.

Today, as always, the audience was transfixed as he spoke. The synagogue ruler was normally diligent to ensure that no-one who was ceremonially unclean entered the synagogue but today, a man with a "spirit of an unclean demon" had entered undetected. Soon enough, the demonic powers that held the man in his life of misery cried out in fear, using the man's voice: ". . . we know who you are!" The Rabbinical cure for demon possession commonly involved drawing out the demon through the nostrils and inviting the demon to either make a splash in a bowl of water or to knock the bowl over as evidence of its departure from the victim: a lengthy process involving complex incantations. But Jesus was the king. Jesus was the one before whom all evil must bow. There was no higher court of appeal. The king had come, and with a mere word of rebuke from him the demon departed and the man sat attentively through the rest of the sermon. The people were amazed.

In the midst of the slow moving crowds making their way home after the service for a delicious Sabbath meal, one man is running. It is Peter. He had left his wife at home that morning to mop her mother's fevered brow. Peter arrives home to find his mother-in-law in bed and delirious with a soaring temperature. The affliction has got dangerously out of control and Peter's wife is beside herself with worry. No cooking aromas fill this home. Jesus comes through the door. The rabbinical method for curing a fever was to tie an iron knife with a lock of hair to a thorn bush, for three days recite verses from the burning bush passage to it, then cut the bush down and burn it. Jesus, with unflustered simplicity and unassailable authority, commands the fever to leave her. Immediately, the woman's temperature returns to normal, the delirium departs and strength fills her muscles. She looks around at them as though cross. What were they all doing standing around when there was a big Sabbath meal to serve?

Jesus has a good few hours of fellowship and laughter as he reclines at table with Peter's extended family. All the while, a district is on the move. Capernaum is a pretty and pleasant place surrounded by green hills and nestling in a natural bay of that big wide freshwater sea. But now, the hidden face of Capernaum and its surrounds is showing itself. Disfigured and tortured sufferers, assisted by loved ones, make their way painfully through the streets in the late afternoon sun to Peter's house. There they will wait until the Sabbath finishes at sunset. They hope that, the day of rest being ended, this rabbi from Nazareth will be willing to work his amazing miracles in their lives. The gathering throng is augmented by sick people from miles around who have been lodging in Capernaum with a view to visiting the healing springs of Tiberias. Out of curiosity, onlookers also gather. Peter's family could hear the voices outside but Jesus was happy, on this occasion, to observe Sabbath custom and wait until sundown before venturing out to them. In the meantime, he does not retire to prepare himself in prayer, but continues to recline with Peter's family.

Finally, Jesus emerges, and heaven touches earth. Men light torches to illuminate this small section of street outside Peter's home and within that glow life after life is set free. People who had never known what normal felt like, are rejoicing in their normality. Others that had been captive to the spiritual torments of trying to bear the yoke of the law plus the traditions of the elders are set free with the touch of his hand. People on stretchers at death's door arise and leap for joy. The blind receive their sight. All night long with a mere word from his mouth or the lightest touch from his hand, hell is emptied. The king has come, and with shrieks of terror, evil is fleeing before his face.

Dawn found Jesus by himself in prayer. His disciples came to him and wanted him to return. He said, "I must preach the kingdom of God to the other cities also . . ." In this phrase, "kingdom of God" was the explanation that all the miracles were illustrations of. It meant two things. The kingdom message pointed to the presence of the king himself. The longed-for messiah had now begun his reign and, though the Romans were still in charge for now, things would never be the same again. Secondly, the kingdom message pointed to what was thought to be the "age to come." With these miraculous events was an in-breaking of the age to come into this present age. It was the presence of the future, an unleashing of the powers of the age to come.

Text: Luke 4:31–43

Prayer: King Jesus, though we still await the day when your rule and reign are not resisted, I welcome your reign in my life and with regards to that situation that is uppermost in my mind right now, I say with all my heart: your kingdom come, powers of a future age break in, God of the breakthrough burst the fetters of evil. Amen.

The Twelve

John the Baptist was already in prison and in Jesus' own ministry murderous opposition had already arisen in his home town. Added to this were the growing numbers of Pharisees and scribes that were travelling up from Jerusalem to infiltrate the crowds of locals and of the somewhat more benign Galilean Pharisees that regularly heard Jesus speak. All of this was prophetic of a slowly gathering storm and Christ, though presently enjoying a fruitful first year of ministry, knew with increasing clarity what fate awaited him. It was already time to begin in earnest the task of investing himself in a small group of followers whose task it would be to safeguard and propagate the good news after his departure.

So it was that, after a night in prayer on a high hill overlooking the Sea of Galilee, Jesus made one of the most momentous decisions of his ministry, without which the Church would probably never have come into existence. He and his Father were already clear that he should keep those six followers of John the Baptist that had been with him since those few days beside the Jordan after his wilderness temptations. They were Peter and Andrew, James and John, and Philip and Batholomew ("Nathanael" in John's Gospel). Added to these would be Matthew the tax collector from the Capernaum seaside booth who Jesus had recently summoned. Jesus further added these five: Thomas, James the Less (or "little"), Judas Lebbaeus Thaddaeus (all one name), Simon the Zealot, and Judas of Kerioth (or "Iscariot"), the only non-Galilean apostle.

The Gospels are all about Christ, so it is unsurprising that nothing but the barest sketches are given of these men. But a number of things can be said. In this group was an uncommon spectrum of political allegiance, temperament and socio-economic standing. Of political allegiance because it included the freedom-fighter Simon who, if he had not himself killed any Roman soldiers, would have approved of anyone who had. He was a terrorist. Yet eating with him every day was Matthew the tax collector for the Romans: a person, naturally speaking, of questionable honesty and loyalty and despicable in the eyes of Simon the Zealot. Of temperament because, sat beside the passionate Peter would be the contemplative John, the emotional Judas Lebbaeus (from *lev* meaning "heart") Thaddaeus (from *thodah* meaning "praise"), and the reticent Thomas. Yet John the mystic also shared with his brother James the epithet Boanerges: "Sons of Thunder." So, within John, and possibly within James also, were a rare combination of the tender and the strong, the contemplative and the passionate. Of socio-economic standing because John and James' father, Zebedee, had hired servants and John knew some important people in Jerusalem (John 18:15) where he had a second home. Similarly, Matthew could throw a sumptuous banquet in his house in honor of Jesus. The rest we may assume to be of humbler means, though no detail is given.

The only thing about the selection of this group that seems exclusive is the fact that so many of them were related: not just to one another but to Jesus himself. Not only were James and John, and Peter and Andrew respectively, brothers, but James and John were the sons of Mary's sister Salome. They were cousins of Jesus. It is also thought likely that Simon the Zealot had as many as three brothers within this group: Judas Lebbaeus Thaddaeus, and Matthew and Thomas, who were possibly twins. Not only that but all four of these may have been the sons of Mary the wife of Cleopas. There is also the view that this Mary was also a sister to Joseph the earthly father of Jesus. We might think this leaves Judas Iscariot and James the Less out in the cold. Not so. There are reasons for believing that Judas Iscariot was Simon the Zealot's son, who probably shared with his father his patriotic zeal and betrayed Jesus out of bitter disappointment with the kind of Messiah he turned out to be. James the Less may have been Judas Lebbaeus Thaddaeus' son. It does, however, leave Philip and Bartholomew unrelated to anyone within this apostolic circle, and Peter and Andrew related only to each other. Sure, some of these views stray too far into conjecture, but you get the picture.

The selection of these twelve men highlights two things. Firstly, Christ's message not only tolerates, it requires, a diverse spectrum of political allegiance, temperament and socio-economic standing. It does not forbid political loyalties, neither does it forbid extremes of temperament, and neither does it forbid being rich. It requires precisely that we have within our number examples from the far poles and from every place in between. Secondly, faith is more, not less likely, to be reproduced into the lives of those related to us. Christ's message spreads via families, and this despite the fact (of which Jesus was only too painfully aware), that familiarity breeds contempt. Faith spreads in our homes or it does not spread at all.

Text: Matthew 10:1–4; Mark 3:16–19

Prayer: Jesus, in the same way that you embraced extremes in human ideology, temperament and social standing, so may my social circle be enriched with a diversity and difference that glorifies you. And in the same way that you started with relatives, so make your home among mine as I reach out to them today. Amen.

The Sermon of Sermons

The morning on the hill had been momentous. That flush of congratulation had coursed through the souls of these twelve chosen men and they looked at the gathering crowds on the plain below with a new feeling. They were no longer the ministered-to but the ministers. They were now Christ's co-workers; carriers of the same power to heal sick bodies and cast out demons. For now though, they left it to the Master himself to descend the slope and lay hands on the sick and afflicted. They all felt alike a desire to have a go and see God's power flow through them but also a reluctance to do anything unless Jesus gave the command. Sure enough, he glanced behind at them and beckoned for them to come and help.

Christ then took his seat in an elevated position at the head of a natural amphitheater with rising ground on either side of a grassy bowl where the multitudes sat. He opened his mouth. What came out was similar to other messages he had earlier given yet never before had his followers heard him expound so fully on the state and life of those who choose to enter his "kingdom." His words fell upon all with soothing grace and liberating truth. Faces shone with gladness. The truth was setting people free from the yoke of the traditions of the elders. Christ's take on what the law of Moses truly required was deeply refreshing. It felt gracious because it was not a teaching that got itself lost in the detail of casuistry—it was exalted. It was not mean, demanding or debasing. It felt true because it was not a dumbing down of the standards of holiness—quite the reverse. Best of all, it was a teaching that, for those with ears to hear, offered Christ himself as its heart and center. It did not stop at being a refreshing interpretation of the law. It promised the reign of the law-giver himself. It promised the presence of the King at the heart of kingdom living.

The Beatitudes set the tone in this regard. Properly, these were not "blessed attitudes" at all but blessed states of being: blessed because if Christ is welcomed into the heart of those living in these states, he becomes the axis between the present and the future. He guarantees, in the age to come, riches and fullness for the spiritually poor, humble, hungry and thirsty, comfort for mourners, mercy for the merciful, peace to the peacemakers, illumination to the pure in heart, and joy to the persecuted. Yet, these states can be described already, in this age, as "happy," "fortunate," and "to be envied." How so? Because Christ is King not only in the age to come, but in this age also. He blurs the boundary between this age and the age to come. He has already taken his throne, and since giving this utterance, has even gone as far as to defeat death itself. Evil is not yet fully vanquished but the King's influence is growing all the time, just like yeast slowly permeating a loaf, or like a mustard tree slowly growing from tiny beginnings. Already, therefore, the sad can experience the comfort of the age to come. Already, the persecuted taste the joys of the consummation when their vindication will shine like a light. Already, the poor in spirit can know the reign of God. And it is this first beatitude—the promise of God's reign to the poor in spirit—that contains them all. The remaining seven are expositions of this one, and all the descriptions of kingdom lifestyle that follow, are sketches of what it looks like when the poor in spirit welcome his reign.

Text: Matthew 5: 1—7:29

Prayer: King Jesus, I invite you to fully take your place in my life. I acknowledge my poverty of spirit. I have nothing to offer but my absolute need of you. I cannot even follow your teachings unless it is you, Jesus, who reigns in me. Reign over all aspects of my life bringing the deep happiness of the world to come. Amen.

TWO

The Six Trials

Christ's first year of ministry that we have glimpsed in earlier chapters was the high water mark of his fame and popularity. Soon, John the Baptist would be beheaded and in that death was a sign of Christ's own pending death in Jerusalem and from that time onwards he repeatedly warned his disciples that his destiny was to be taken by lawless men, be beaten, mocked and crucified, but that this fate would result in him being in some way a "ransom for many" (Mark 10:45). He also intensified what we would call his succession plan. He sent out the Twelve on their own mission around Galilee and later tried the same thing with seventy. Much to his relief, both missions were a resounding success.

And so he comes to Jerusalem for the last time. For now, he is acclaimed with loud shouts as he rides a donkey through the gates. With a heavy heart he rides into that city laden with history—and full of blood, the blood of the prophets. It was the graveyard of every messenger ever sent to it. And now, one more time there would be one more Messenger proclaiming to it the way of peace. His sorrow was not for himself as he contemplated the inevitable outcome but for the people of that great city who would soon bear the cost of their rejection of God's message and Messenger.

The King of the Jews

In no time at all, Judas betrayed him and he was arrested late at night in the place he loved, a garden on the Mount of Olives.

Before Annas

A nd so begins the night without sleep, of gnawing hunger, and of wave after wave of bullying as the noble king of all bows to his subjects as they brutalize him. There are six trials in all, each one illegal in some way or other and each one adding up to a case so weak that, in the end, he is condemned out of his own mouth, out of something about the nature of his being that he is forced to admit.

The first trial on that cool, starry Spring night was before Annas, the aged, outgoing high priest. His villa was on the way to the house of the reigning high priest Caiaphas, which was the next stop after this. Annas was the one who profited from the money-changing and animal-selling businesses that thrived in the temple courts, whose tables Jesus had kicked over, for the second time in his ministry, only a few days earlier. It was the dead of night when no such trials should have been taking place. There were no witnesses and there was no evidence. Annas calmly asked the bound Jesus about his teaching, about how many disciples he had, anything, in fact, that was so straightforward and reasonable as to lure Jesus into lowering his guard. Then, there would be a question thrown in very suddenly to catch him out. At least that was the plan. The Master's brazen reply: "You should know what I teach, it's common knowledge, I taught openly. Why don't you ask the people who heard me?" was a shock. Annas' assistant responded with protective instinct for his hoary master's honor, slapping Jesus across the face. This provoked Jesus to ask for the thing that was pointedly lacking: evidence that he might actually be guilty of anything.

This slap is an act on the part of the powerful that says, "How dare you be confident?" We might like to think that our world in the West is free of such abominable brutishness. It is the behavior we portray in costume drama: the historic patriarch exploding with rage at his daughter who has grown up too fast and refuses to marry the suitor chosen for her. She brazenly stands up for herself. But these forces are very much with us. Those forces were unleashed at the 2013 Oscars. Janice Turner, in her column for *The Times* described the presenter's song about all the Oscar-winning actresses that have uncovered their breasts on screen as an, "elaborate and calculated insult."[1] How dare these actresses receive due recognition for decades of acting achievement? Let's reduce all that success to nothing more than mammary glands. It can be compared to the strike of Annas' servant, and the dismay from the blow was visible on the faces of many of the actresses as their names were reeled off in song in front of family, colleagues and 1 billion viewers.

Satan himself is described as the accuser. He hates the head held high, loathes the shame-free life and hits out at human achievement. Maybe you have felt his blows. Defy him today.

Text: John 18:13, 19–24

Application: Revelation 12:10–12

Prayer: Father, in the name of your Son, thank you that I, like He, can be confident in the face of intimidating people, words or circumstances. Even my own conscience may accuse me, but I take my stand with the unashamed and hold my head high in the righteousness of Christ. Amen

---

1. Turner, "A Casting Couch Only Works in a Locked Room," 25.

Before Caiaphas

Think of the phrase, "Guantanamo Bay" and you think of people arrested and detained without charge, of people being forced to wear bright orange boiler suits and being subjected to interminable abuse that supposedly stops just short of torture according to Geneva Convention definitions. A newborn son back home is a six year-old school boy by the time his innocent father is released. Years are wasted as interrogators try to extract information that confirms a teetering pile of prejudice and supposition that they call "intelligence." I am speaking of an Algerian restaurateur who, in 2002, was arrested because he went to Afghanistan to cook road-side meals for fleeing Afghan refugees. In 2007 he is finally told, "You're free to go," and is sent back home without explanation and without apology.[2] The account of his experience, called *The General* has now come out as a book. Clearly we are, and always have been, a lot better at prejudice and hate than we are at justice. Guantanamo Bay simply reminds us that injustice can be at its most brutal when lurking behind the hypocritical veneers of Western powers.

Turn back the clock two thousand years. It is about 4am, and Sanhedrin members are being woken up and are gradually starting to assemble at the house of Caiaphas, the reigning High Priest. Annas, knowing this, decides he is finished with Jesus and sends him there. There is a more or less private interview with Caiaphas, though with a growing number of priests and lawyers assembling. The first glow of daylight this chilly morning is still another hour

2. Whittell, "Prisoner 590, Guantanamo Bay," 26–32

23

away and not until dawn would it be legal to hold a full trial before the whole Sanhedrin. Jesus at this stage is still without charge and is being held for no sound reason. Caiaphas begins his interrogation in a way that echoes that of Annas but with rather more of a note of urgency borne of self-interest. Caiaphas, after all, is the one that had arranged the arrest and, with the great and the good of Jerusalem now gathering, he must elicit from reliable witnesses the reasons for waking everyone up. He is already playing fast and loose with the law in planning for a trial to take place on the same day that evidence is taken, now he is going to try to hurry some good-enough-sounding evidence through the system. It is Guantanamo-style hypocrisy: following something vaguely like due process but with a heart full of disdain. The most likely charge to stick would be blasphemy, based on Leviticus 24:16, but the best the witnesses could come up with were two inconsistent reports about Jesus recommending that the temple be destroyed and offering the promise that he would rebuild it in three days.

The Scriptures, however, at least in the way the ruling Sadducees interpreted them, did allow a person to be condemned out of their own mouth. There is, for example, the occasion when Joshua extracted a confession from Achan by placing him under oath. Matthew records Caiaphas doing exactly that here. Jesus' response must have been music to the scheming High Priest's ears. It was just perfect; better than expected after so much stonewalling by the prisoner, a sheer gift for a man whose chief passion was his own reputation: "Are you the Christ, the Son of the Blessed?" "I am. And hereafter you will see the Son of Man sitting at the right hand of the Power and coming with the clouds of heaven."

In the distance, a cock crows. Peter has just denied three times that he even knows him. Then, in a superb display of piety, Caiaphas tears his robe in two. Some of those gathered with Caiaphas take their opportunity to slap, punch and spit on Jesus as he is led away to a pack of hungry dogs: bored soldiers who, just like the guards of Guantanamo or the soldiers of Abu Ghraib have switched off their humanity. He is blind-folded and slapped again and again. Legend had it that the Messiah would be able to perceive things purely by his sense of smell (based on Isa 11:3), so they say, "Prophesy to us, Christ: who hit you?" The second trial was over, four more await.

OK, so it's awful, it's a miscarriage of justice of just the kind we hear about all the time, an atrocity, an outrage. It is easy to draw parallels with the present day precisely because the scene—at least via the media—is such a familiar one to us: a scene of oppression and abuse. There is one thing and only one thing that is completely odd about this story. It is the silence of the accused, the complete absence of rage. The Algerian restaurateur was known for his rage while in detention. He acquired the nick-name, The General, because of his ability to rally all the other prisoners in acts of combined defiance and aggression against the guards. But here in Jesus we see no warrior. We see someone who exercises his right to remain silent until, under oath to his Father, he is made to speak up and duly throws Caiaphas a lifeline.

No one wants to be a doormat and I would never advise anyone that they need to be. Yet the practice of silence in the face of provocation, accusation, or any other kind of pressure, is a discipline worth perfecting. The interesting thing to note about most of our rages is their sheer triviality. As we let this scene of Jesus before Caiaphas cast its shadow across road rage for instance, it is shown up for its true petulant colors. Whether our provocations are on the scale of a defiant toddler and a time to be out the door or on a par with Guantanamo and years of your life lost to a huge miscarriage of justice, it would do no harm for the noble silence of the Christ to be the first thing we think of, rather than the last.

Text: Matthew 26:57–75; Mark 14:53–72; Luke 22:54; John 18:24

Application: 1 Peter 3:8–10; Philippians 2:14–15

Prayer: Lord Jesus, you are already there with me in those moments, those flash points, those times of the day when I am most likely to lose patience. Stand by me in that moment and let there be the power to respond like you would. Amen.

Before the Sanhedrin

Imagine yourself in an airport. It is not some big fancy airport with plenty of diversions. It is small and regional and your flight is delayed. It is five o'clock in the morning and you have had no sleep, you have no currency, your books are read and the orange tints of dawn are streaking across the sky. Your teeth need brushing and you are desperately tired. Supposing then that airport security descended upon you. Two officers, armed, walk up to you. One approaches at your left and the other at your right, as though expecting trouble. They escort you brusquely to an interrogation room where you are presented with a bag you have never seen with white powder inside. You are in a country where possessing narcotics is a capital offense.

The third trial of Jesus is at dawn. He has been slapped about. He has had no sleep, nothing to drink and no food. Now, it is time for the grand official ratification of the verdict that Caiaphas had already extracted from Jesus' own words. The minimum seventy Sanhedrin members are present and the sentence of death is passed. It is clinical—ill-founded, illegal—but official, awaiting only the validation of the Roman Procurator, the murderous Pontius Pilate. As with the previous trial, Jesus hands sentence to Caiaphas on a plate: "You are right in saying that I am" (Luke 22:70).

Thus the third trial concludes as the trumpets resound announcing the sunrise and a perfect Passover lamb is slaughtered in the temple. As Jim Bishop said, "This day began with an old sacrifice. It would end with a new one."[3] For Jesus, the wrestling

3. Bishop, *The Day Christ Died*, 221.

was long past. The outcome of the night had already been decided the moment he uttered these words before his arrest: "Nevertheless, not my will but yours be done." The sentiment of those private words with his Father was now expressed in these public words before Caiaphas: "It is as you say." Thus the last of the three Jewish trials concludes with the consent of the God-Man to face judgment from those whom he ought to judge. Here, God passes sentence upon himself. God gives His verbal assent to be the bearer of judgment rather than the bringer of it. In the few words of Christ's final hours hang the destiny of the human race.

Text: Matthew 27:1; Mark 15:1

Application: 1 Peter 3:15–18

Prayer: Thank you Lord, for standing up for me during your trials. Thank you for resolutely going ahead with the sacrifice that was going to save me. Thank you for saving me. Amen.

Before Pilate

His hair is matted. His face is swollen with bruises. His body has not been allowed to recoup except perhaps in the hour or two in custody that must have elapsed between his early morning trial before the Sanhedrin and the opening of his trial before Pilate. During this interval, Caiaphas continues to work on polishing the legal veneer of the case by having it formally written up. This includes a list of offences against Jewish law and Roman. At some point in the middle of this piece of work Judas re-appears looking shaken and tormented and wishing to return the price he had been paid for Jesus. It is not accepted by the priests since to do so would have required the release of Jesus, so Judas throws the pieces of silver on the floor of the temple, much to the consternation of passers-by. His leather money belt then becomes partly the means for Judas, overcome with anguish, to depart this life. What finally killed him, however, were the rocks of the Kidron Valley upon which he fell when the branch holding the noose broke free.

A large and heavily armed escort surrounded Jesus as he was brought before Pilate. The concealment was so effective that the vast majority of Jesus' followers were still as yet unaware of his arrest and were looking expectantly for some more great teaching to be delivered from temple precincts and steps.

That a case was being hurried through like this on the eve of Passover was unheard of and irritated Pilate. He knew that the motives for such a rush could not possibly be a disinterested concern for justice and he resented being used as the rubber stamp for it. Nevertheless, he had agreed all of this beforehand with Caiaphas and had even committed some of his troops to the task of arresting

Jesus at Gethsemane. So when he professed complete ignorance of the case, Caiaphas was understandably exasperated: "If he were not a criminal we would not have brought him before you."

The confession of Jesus is unswerving, his refusal of lifelines offered to him during the questioning unstinting. This was the hour and the Scriptures must be fulfilled. "Are you then a king?" "It is as you say," is the standard reply given in cases of extreme gravity, a little like our, "'fraid so," only graver. It is not, as some of the English translations might suggest, an evasive reply like, "OK, whatever you say." It is an emphatic "yes," but uttered with full awareness of the seriousness of such a claim in the eyes of a system that acknowledged no king but Caesar. Jesus, however, explains what sort of king he is—not a political king but a king of another world, another order of life altogether but a world that is so immanent as to attract "followers" that don't fight for him.

This time, it looks as though he has got himself off the hook. The answer satisfies Pilate. But, by now, the forces of darkness have gathered. Crowds of brigands have been primed with what to shout and when. Pilate fears a revolt, the fourth on his watch. He would be recalled to Caesar and stripped of his post. Then Pilate grasps at a word: "Galilee." This man is under Herod's jurisdiction, let's send the Galilean peasant king to him.

Text: Matthew 27:2–14; Mark 15:2–5; Luke 23:1–6; John 18:28–38

Application: 1 Timothy 6:12–14

Prayer: Thank you Lord for taking a stand when it most mattered. I know that temptations will come my way to compromise my dearest values and that too often before I have caved in. May the same Spirit that strengthened You strengthen me too. Amen.

Before Herod

With the admission of Jesus and his small entourage of enemies into the glorious white marble palace of Herod Antipas, the trials take on a new complexion. Angry courtroom intimidation will now turn into belittlement and mockery. The stonewalling will continue but will be responded to with laughter rather than solemn oaths.

Herod is courteous, offering his new guests some comfortable places to sit while he sets about the task of getting Jesus to perform a miracle for everyone's entertainment. If any of the trials come close to mirroring what our culture does with Jesus, it is this one. The objective is not justice but entertainment, not truth but sport. This is what it looks like when a culture of levity meets a perfect person: they array him in a gorgeous silken robe and, to roars of laughter, bow the knee and pay mock homage.

This trial is unique in that Jesus, throughout this brief audience with a puppet king, utters not one word. In the case of the other trials, though fully exercising his right to remain silent, he does answer for himself as the occasion demands. In front of Herod, himself a mock king, a charade of a monarch and not even fully Jewish, Jesus stands and stares at the wall behind. Herod is in playful mood but is feeling humiliated in front of his courtiers. The chief priests who came with Jesus keep interrupting the questioning with loud accusations, which only further add to Herod's irritation. Again and again he has to ask them to be quiet. The trial ends with the fake king projecting onto the true Davidic king his own inauthenticity, sending him back to Pilate dressed up in royal costume.

This trial speaks a serious diagnosis to our culture. It encapsulates too perfectly what we would do with Jesus and warns too clearly of what he would do with us. Jesus be not silent with us your loudest mockers.

Text: Luke 23:7–12

Application: Romans 12:19–21

Prayer: Today, I separate myself from the cynicism of our age and say, I believe in You Lord Jesus and I ask you to take your place, without rival, as the Lord of my heart. Amen.

Before Pilate Again

Pilate was a man answerable to Tiberius Caesar. Tiberius was a man who is described by Tacitus as covered in spots and emitting a strange smell. Externals aside he was an interesting emperor: not just another grape-eating, goblet-quaffing hedonist. He was staunchly democratic, seeking to restore the principles of the original Roman Republic. He was scholarly and completely devoid of emotion. The damage to his emotions probably arose from having been forced, for political reasons, to divorce his sweetheart and only confidant and enter instead upon a loveless marriage. He was keen to preserve peace throughout the empire and was outraged by any reports of governors mistreating subject peoples. He was a hands-on administrator who needed to keep the likes of Pilate in constant fear of being recalled to Rome. He had informers.

Pilate for his part had, by the time he faced the King of the Jews, narrowly escaped the full wrath of Tiberius three times already. He had upset the Jews by installing in Jerusalem the Roman flag that bore the image of the emperor at a time when emperor worship was being expected. The Jews, not fearing death at his hands, blackmailed him into removing them. He had gone on to hang Roman shields on the walls of the Antonia Fortress. This provoked a riot, which was violently suppressed. The Jews then wrote to Tiberius to complain, incurring an angry letter to Pilate from the emperor. Lastly, he had used excessive force against a group of Samaritans, which got him in trouble with his immediate superior: the governor of Syria. Pilate had had his innate stubbornness badly shaken. When this mob gathered at his doorstep loudly demanding the crucifixion of a controversial rabbi, he knew his career was at stake. At literally any cost, he must avoid a riot.

With Jesus now standing once again before him and the priesthood again accusing him we see Pilate clutch at three successive straws, all of which he hoped would absolve him from having to judge this case at all. He had, in fact, already acquitted Jesus, but then effectively re-opened the case by sending him to Herod. Jesus had come back from Herod wearing a robe that signaled that Herod likewise was not willing to judge the case but only to mock the man. Out of Herod's sloped shoulders Pilate tries to wrest a victory by pointing out to the accusers that Herod had effectively agreed with him that Jesus posed no real threat and had done nothing worthy of the death penalty. This was his first straw.

The gathering mob will not accept this and Pilate, despite finding Jesus not guilty, throws out a fatal line: "I will therefore chastise him and let him go." Not only is this unjust if Jesus is not guilty, it shows that he is weakening. He is trying to have it both ways: please the crowds and let him go. By now, his wife, Claudia, had warned him not to have anything to do with condemning Jesus. But Pilate foolishly holds onto this punish-and-release option to the bitter end, hoping that the pathetic sight of a badly whipped man would be enough to convince the crowds to let him go. In the meantime a third straw comes his way as he dimly picks up the word "Barabbas" among the many things the mob is shouting.

Among those who had been primed with what to shout are those whose desires are more genuine. These are the relatives of Jesus Barabbas, a man arrested for murder and insurrection but who had not yet been sentenced. They are calling for Pilate to invoke the Festival Amnesty: the custom of releasing one un-sentenced prisoner during festival seasons such as Passover. Pilate tries to turn this to his advantage hoping that, if faced with the alternatives: release a brigand or release a gentle rabbi, they would be forced to choose what is right.

The priests whip up the crowds who all cry out with venom that is shocking and threatening: "Crucify him! Release Barabbas!" Almost inevitably, given Pilate's history of getting himself into trouble with Tiberius, the blackmailing soon begins: "If you release Barabbas you are no friend of Caesar. Whoever makes himself a king is an enemy of Caesar." This sudden and touching loyalty to the emperor is an obvious pretense but the threat implied is clearly no idle one.

Finally, Pilate resorts to the second straw in a modified form: have him flogged but then present him to the mob for them to decide who lives and who dies. Some listless Syrian soldiers are waiting. These recruits were made constantly unwelcome by the Jews. They in turn had no respect for the Jewish people. This flogging, therefore, is partly an act of heartfelt anti-Semitism and partly an act of duty. Atop a short pillar no more than three feet high would be two iron hooks to which the prisoner's wrists were tied. Pieces of chain and bone, and perhaps iron balls, were tied into strings of leather, which were held together by a wooden handle. Two channels either side of the pillar disposed of the blood. Despite the half hour long flagellation scene in *The Passion of the Christ,* a whipping of this severity was too life-threatening to go on for longer than a few minutes. Many victims passed out after the first stroke. The flogging would be carefully supervised to ensure the victim was still alive, however faintly, at the end. By the time the flogging of Jesus ceases, he is semi-conscious, his body in shock. He is unable to stand un-assisted and is shaking all over. The way that Herod had returned him in a kingly robe gave the soldiers an idea. They too find a majestic cape, this time a military one, but they go further still, finding some thorny brush that had been piled up for making fires. The spikes of this particular bush—a nuisance of a weed—were very long, and the branches supple enough to be twisted into a crown. He keeps collapsing but eventually recovers enough to stand and be duly arrayed and crowned, complete with a staff to hold in his hand. His flayed nerve endings are now recovering from their numbness to send signals of intense pain from almost everywhere on the surface of his body. Some of the whipping has caught his face.

Tottering and red with blood, the thorn-crowned king is presented: "Behold, your king!" One more attempt to reason with the crowds yields the revelation that he is the Son of God. It becomes clear that an accusation of blasphemy (Son of God) had weirdly mutated into one of high treason (King of the Jews). Only now did Pilate know of the original accusation. Pilate is afraid. He had heard of gods coming to earth and some deep superstitions were being awakened. There is one last interview and further pleadings. It is no use. A riot is imminent. Barabbas is released and Jesus is led away to be crucified. So ends the sixth and final trial. It is now approaching midday. Within three hours Jesus would be dead.

Self-interest is the main characteristic of this trial, not only Pilate's concern for his livelihood but also that of the priesthood. Jesus' message was understood to be primarily an anti-temple polemic. In a nation of abject poverty, a priesthood that thrived on a generous portion of everyone's meat and cereal offerings felt understandably threatened by a rabbi who taught people to call God their Father and pray prayers that could move mountains—without the mediation of a priest.

In these six trials we see the worst in human nature and the best, as it were, in divine nature. In the first trial (before Annas), intimidation meets confidence. In the second trial (before Caiaphas), coercion meets open confession and in the third, the hypocrisy of Caiaphas before the Sanhedrin meets rock-steady integrity. The fourth trial (before Pilate) shows what cowardice looks like as it meets courage. Fifthly, before Herod mockery meets silence and in this final trial self-interest meets the driving force that has led the Son of God through all the trials to this climactic moment: love. This was not an "if" kind of love, nor yet a "because" love—there was nothing to warrant that, no possible cause for this kind of love. It was a full-orbed "in spite of" love, a "nevertheless" love. In the face of every reason to hate us, Jesus loved. Jesus was, to quote Jim Packer, "moved by a love that was determined to do everything necessary to save us."[4] Why such horrors were necessary for our salvation is the subject of atonement theology. Thankfully, the facts themselves speak to our spirits and move us at a level

---

4. Packer, "What Did the Cross Achieve?" 25.

much deeper than theology, but to which the best of our theology, stammering and awe-struck, tries to give grateful expression.

Text: Matthew 27:15–31; Mark 15:6–20; Luke 23:13–25; John 18:39—19:16

Application: 1 John 3:16

Prayer: Lord, give me an opportunity today to show your self-giving love towards someone that has done nothing to deserve it. Amen.

THREE

Seven Sayings

And so the last trial becomes the first of the fourteen "stations" of the cross. Before we get to hear the first of the seven unforgettable sayings of Jesus from the cross, there are a further ten stations. However, there is, in fact, so little biblical information about what happened in between Christ being sentenced to death and his being finally nailed to the cross that only four of the ten stations describing his agonizing journey to Golgotha are of biblical origin. The rest (the three "falls," meeting his mother, Veronica wiping his face and the stripping of his clothes) are traditional, though in some cases, strongly implied by the biblical account. The three biblical stations are: the carrying of the cross, the co-opting of Simon of Cyrene to help carry the cross, meeting the women of Jerusalem and the nailing to the cross. The remaining stations describe the death, the taking down of the body from the cross and the entombment.

"Father Forgive Them . . ."

The eleventh station then, is the nailing of Jesus to the cross. First comes the knee of a soldier pressing his right arm into place against the course wood of the *patibulum* as Jesus lies there beneath the midday skies. Next comes the thumb of the executioner feeling for the little hollow in the wrist that is created by the parting of the two bones of the lower arm just before they fuse at the wrist. This fusing will be useful for suspending the weight of the prisoner later on. Now, He can feel the tip of the square cut six-inch nail being placed where the executioner's thumb had been. He is very swift. He has done hundreds of crucifixions before and is deaf to the irrepressible cry of Jesus as the iron mallet-head is brought down with full force upon the nail. This agony will be repeated twice as the Carpenter is helplessly attached to wood. First his wrists are pinned to the cross beam, then, after hoisting, his feet are pinned to the upright that is already in the ground. Thus, in no time at all and with masterful efficiency, he finds himself suspended just a foot or so off the ground, with two criminals either side. The conclusion of a night of abuse and injustice is that no one has spoken up for him. No one has come to the rescue—despite his popularity with the common people. In the midst of a nation that prided itself on being more righteous than any of its neighbors and under the jurisdiction of an empire whose justice system was the envy of the world, the Holy One is left to die. He is delivered over to a method of execution that had been perfected over 600 years. It was designed to be not too quick, but not so ineffectual that there was any likelihood of survival: inevitable but slow—and as humiliating as possible so that others would learn from it. From it we get three English words: "excruciating" (literally, "from a cross"), "crux"—something utterly central, and "crucial" (literally, "cross-shaped")—something indispensable.

An entirely normal thing would be a cry of rage, like the two thieves. He seemed to have been rendered powerless. Why does he not, if physical strength will allow, start one of his stirring speeches about "hypocrites" now? Between gasps, maybe. Or why not call on those twelve legions of angels? It is at this point that one of the most remarkable of the seven saying of Jesus from the cross is uttered. He raises himself up on the nails, and in a voice that all can hear: priesthood, executioners, passers-by, mockers, cries out: "Father, forgive them for they know not what they do!" He sinks down again, a great donation of words given to the Father and thrown to the heedless world below.

Jesus is entirely consistent with himself, having so famously taught that followers must love their enemies and pray for them. He is fulfilling Scripture. Isaiah had prophesied long ago that the Messiah would make intercession for transgressors. He intercedes for "them"—all who had a hand in his crucifixion. And he acknowledges that they don't know "what" they do. They don't understand the full significance of it.

There is not much to say about this before we immediately, and quite rightly, find ourselves turning towards the state of our own hearts. Our "them" must likewise include all those that have offended us, not just those that we deem to be the more excusable. Even the inexcusable, even those that have betrayed their own values so deeply that we say, "I don't know how they sleep at night!" Our "what" is likewise something that we can be sure the perpetrators had no idea about. They knew what they did—what they said, what they implied, what they had engineered—but not the full significance of the "what." They had no idea that it destroyed us. It need destroy us no more. Remember the adage: it could make you better instead of bitter. Forgiving could be the making of you.

Text: Luke 23:34

Prayer: Father, forgive all the people that have hurt me the most. They did not know what they did. I entrust myself to you. Amen.

"Today you will be with me"

The second saying of Jesus also belongs to those moments just at the start of his three hours suspended on the cross when the physical pain is at its height. They are clipped sentences utterable only as the result of enormous effort as Christ lifts himself up on his nails in order to be able to exhale and hence to speak.

At this point we find ourselves almost back inside Herod's court. Luke, in particular, paints a picture of a growing torrent of abuse. Jesus seems to be surrounded by cynical, unbelieving mockery and cruel jibes.

Two things cause the jeering. The biggest cause is that this is a nation that is tired of belief. It is a nation that God had judged by sending them into exile for a time. After a couple of generations, the Persians allowed them to start trickling back to Palestine to re-build Jerusalem and their lives, though many had made a good life right where they were and stayed. Then, when the Persians were defeated by the Greeks there was a new imperial power dominating the Mediterranean basin: Alexander the Great and his vast acquisitions of territory. When his kingdom was divided into four, Israel became the battle ground between two rival successors of Alexander the Great, passing every few years under the jurisdiction of one mini-empire, then the other. There was a brief interlude when, while Greek power was weak, their yoke was thrown off, but then came the Romans: same old story. Despair crept over the people. They could not understand: they had repented of all the things they had been judged for in exile yet seemingly God was not willing that they should truly return from that exile. Instead, though living in their own land, they were subject to one foreign oppressor after another. Many wrote great apocalyptic visions at this time that, in the manner of the book of Daniel, predicted the coming of a great messianic figure who would take vengeance on their enemies and finally vindicate the righteous. The irritating thing was that there was no shortage of people popping up all over the place claiming to be the long-awaited Messiah. Yet they all turned out to be charlatans. It is partly in this context of a nation weary of believing and tired of hoping that some of the mockery of Jesus becomes so venomous.

Similarly, in our culture, we have learned that believing in big ideas and total solutions to the ills of our race is not worth pursuing. It leads only to wars. The great clash of competing ideologies that was World War II still scars us as a people. And so, we don't believe in "science and progress" anymore, or any of the big ideas of modernity. We have become tongue-in-cheek about everything. Nobody wants to be too earnest and the earnest are likely to be mocked. We are weary and wary of belief.

The other cause of the jeering was the sign posted above Jesus' head: "This is Jesus, the King of the Jews." The religious authorities were fearful that there might be some non-cynics passing by that might read it and be inclined to believe it. Hence, they were very hot-under-the-collar about the way Pilate had chosen to phrase the sign as though it were a statement of fact: this man really is the King. They rushed to Pilate urging him to rephrase it but Pilate, still smarting from the trial, wasn't about to give way on that one.

Hence there is a little row of priests standing by the road who, every time there is a passing gaggle of late-arriving Passover pilgrims, start shouting things like, "Let the King come down now from the cross and we will believe him!" One of the criminals crucified with Jesus joins in the taunt, "Yeah, if you're the King, save yourself and us!" The passing pilgrims are soon enough convinced and make a few rude gestures at the King of the Jews before continuing on their way to the city gate. Another few pass by and the priests repeat the same routine.

Just as before Herod the comedian king, Christ's response to the mockery is silence, silence that is, until there comes his way just one little overture of faith. It comes from the stranger next to him on the other cross. Jesus can hear him raise himself up, snorting through sweat and pain as he does so, and gathering the strength to shout back at the other crucified stranger who has just jeered at Jesus: "Do you not fear God? We are only getting what we deserve but this man has done nothing wrong!" There is no response from the man. He has sunk down and seems not to hear. Then this unbidden defendant of the innocence of Jesus adds: "Lord, remember me when you come into your kingdom." Jesus prizes this one step of faith that has beautifully crowned the very closing moments of an otherwise hideous life: "Assuredly I say to you, today you will be with me in Paradise." The faithful stranger is welcomed into an eternity at home with Christ.

Text: Luke 23:43

Prayer: Lord, you have welcomed me as one of your own. May life today be an extension of your welcoming love to a stranger. Amen.

"Behold Your Son"

Imagine you are in great pain yourself, whether emotional or physical and then your eyes light upon someone close to you who is in need of what you alone can give. Or supposing you are in a caring profession. It is your job to care. You are paid to care. Yet this particular day, something has come your way that has put you in great need of care and attention from someone yourself. Then, into your office or your surgery comes someone with a much lesser problem than your own, looking to you for compassion, for guidance. These can be moments that test our maturity. These are times that test our others-centeredness.

And this kind of moment is the one we witness as we hear the third utterance from the cross. It is the last in a group that are all uttered at the start of his three hours upon the cross when the physical pain is at its height. Later, there will be the danger of slipping into unconsciousness so, while he is fully alert, he must meet the needs of those around him and tidy up his affairs. He has met a need for forgiveness. He has extended mercy and hospitality to the stranger on the cross next to his. Now, out of that same well of love, not blocked by bitterness, he says goodbye to his mother and his closest friend. In line with all the other words from the cross, we have here not a long tear-soaked farewell but a couple of clipped phrases said in great pain while suspending himself on his nails: "Mother, behold your son; son, behold your mother." John, as we saw, was Jesus' cousin in any case, so here an auntie and a nephew take care of each other. This was a very sensible arrangement, but one that pointedly includes no mention of Christ's siblings. Jesus had, as far as we know, four younger brothers and a number of sisters who could have cared for their mother after the death of the eldest (we assume Joseph had passed away by now). Their attitude until now, however, had been skeptical and unbelieving. It seems Jesus wanted his mother cared for within the believing community of followers.

This saying, like the previous two, is a cameo of Christ's character. If we had any doubts about how perfect he was while reading about his miracles and ministry, we see here at the cross the character of the Christ shining more brightly than ever. Here, in spite of immense reasons for rage, he forgives, in spite of an arsenal of reasons not to welcome the stranger, he does, and in spite of his own unbearable pain, he reaches out to his nearest and dearest, not for sympathy, but to meet their needs.

Text: John 19:26–27

Prayer: Jesus, to aspire towards the hero quality of others-centeredness is an easy thing; but the reality seems elusive and far off. Grow me into just such a person, I pray. Start today with a chance for me to reach out to someone whose need might seem smaller than my own. Amen.

"My God, my God, why . . . ?"

Tom Hanks is one of my favorite actors. He is one of those movie stars that have almost never appeared in a duff movie. One particularly memorable one belonged to the now fairly well established sub-genre of survival stories—films of the eating insects, growing a long beard and going half-crazy type. The film, of course, is *Castaway.* He is part of a small crew manning a FedEx cargo flight. In a storm the plane goes down on an uninhabited tropical island with the loss of all the other lives on board. He goes for a walk up the island's only mountain and discovers that he is indeed quite alone and surrounded on all sides by ocean. And yes, he grows a beard and learns to spear fish. Then the loneliness sets in. Cargo from the plane is strewn all over the beach and among the debris is a ball. He manages to paint a face on it and puts it on a pole. It is his friend. He talks to it day and night, and when at last he finishes building a raft he takes it on board with him. He has got quite a way from land when suddenly the ball falls overboard. It has become his only friend so he dives in and tries to swim after it. In despair he watches it drift further and further away from him. Looking back he can see that he himself is now getting further away from the raft. He comes to himself and swims back to the raft only to burst into tears over the loss of the only thing that had relieved the unrelenting solitude for so many months. Eventually, he is picked up by a passing oil tanker.

Of the same sub-genre is another excellent film: *127 Days.* It is the story of a young man who goes rock climbing in an arid desert. He is clearly extremely adept at leaping across rocks yet is so over-confident he has set off for his hike without telling a soul where he is going and without any means of contacting anyone. He falls down a deep ravine and finds that he has got his hand irretrievably stuck between two very large rocks. He struggles constantly to get free. He then manages to drop what little was left of his water supply and watches it spill out onto the bottom of the ravine. After a while, he becomes delirious and thinks he is in a radio interview recounting his experience. Then, he dreams that it starts to rain and the ravine fills with wonderful cool water that washes him free. Then he awakes to find that it has not rained and he is still stuck. Eventually, he takes the decision to sever his own hand with a pen knife while biting on some clothing to deal with the pain. He gets free and manages to find some hikers who come to his aid.

These kinds of stories provide us with a window into absolute aloneness. They remind us of how difficult it is to survive in total isolation. The solitude always seems to have a maddening effect. And it is this absolute loneliness that the fourth word from the cross is about: "My God, my God, why have you forsaken me?" The first three utterances were about contrast. There was the contrast between the callous self-interest of those that crucified Jesus and his cry to the Father for their forgiveness. There was the contrast between the sea of jeering that engulfs the scene and the one overture of faith that we hear from the criminal on the cross, and further, Christ's silence towards those who mocked and his immediate and full response to the one who believed. And lastly, we saw the contrast between Christ's intense personal pain and his care for his nearest and dearest. Instead of digging for sympathy, he bids them approach the cross and gives simple, unsentimental instructions about how he wished his mother's needs to be met after his departure. Now, however, we move from contrast to contradiction. Darkness has descended upon the hill and the one who had once said, "I and my Father are one," now, from the midst of the darkness says, "My God, my God, why have you forsaken me?"

Here, we approach the edge of a bottomless pit of unfathomable meaning. As we approach the hole, two words are of some help in deciphering what is happening here. The first one is "you."

Jesus had endured opposition from humankind and the buffeting of Satan, but now it was God the Father himself that seemed to have in some way turned his face from Christ: ". . . why have *you* forsaken me?" Then, as we alight on the word "me" we note the trajectory that began in Gethsemane and Christ's total commitment to do the Father's will even in the face of overwhelming reasons not to obey. That trajectory of obedience had brought him all the way through the trials, the scourging and the crucifying to this point and still his obedience was unwavering. So why would the Father desert him now: his obedient Son? ". . . why have you forsaken *me*?" It is not until we look at the word "why" though, that we find that we have approached the black hole and are staring down it with him: Why?

Jürgen Möltmann is widely regarded as one of the greatest theologians of our age yet his theological journey began at precisely this place. He and his close friend were manning an anti-aircraft battery during an allied air raid on East Hamburg. One night he saw his friend blown to pieces by a bomb though he himself was miraculously unscathed. There and then he knelt down in the darkness and smoldering devastation and said, "My God, where are you?" He had not thought much about God until then. Later on in the war he was captured and taken to three prisoner of war camps in Britain, finally ending up in Kilmarnock where some Dutch missionaries, overcoming their natural hatred for the Nazis, arrived and distributed Bibles, telling the prisoners all about Jesus. It was there also that Möltmann was shown pictures of Belsen and Auschwitz and came to the heart-rending realization, amid so much loss, that the regime he had been fighting for had not been worth the effort. He had fought for a bunch of criminals. Back in Germany, amid the devastation, he and a number of veteran theologians gathered to teach theology but found that the only place they could start was with this cry of dereliction. The cross became the heart and center of Möltmann's thought. The cross, with all its contradiction and mystery was, for him, the test of any theology that would lay claim to being Christian theology. For he reckoned that the godforsaken Christ on the cross was the only God that a suffering and broken world might be able to hear and believe in.

So at the heart and center of this cry from the cross is the heart and center of the event of the cross itself, and the heart and center of Christian faith. Not surprisingly, it speaks very clearly to our world today. I was at a conference recently where one of the papers given was about how our society creates in so many of us an "intimacy deficit." About one in five of us are, at any one time, going through a time of feeling unable to connect with anyone, a time of loneliness. Our culture tends to compensate for the starvation from intimacy by over-emphasizing sex. Sex becomes overloaded with all of our longings for intimacy. We are prone to lust because we are not intimately connected at a deeper level with people. And, when we do enter romantic relationships we load these with exaggerated expectations about what they will give us, resulting in disappointment and divorce.

There is a trajectory that runs, like a fissure in the earth, from Gethsemane on the Mount of Olives, and Christ's pledge of obedience there to this moment on Calvary's hill. But it does not stop there. It goes from here all the way to the Temple Mount where, during an earthquake, the thick double curtain separating the Most Holy Place from the rest of the temple, will very soon be torn in two from top to bottom at the moment when Jesus bows his head and dies. Here is a Man who has come to represent us, obeying at every point where we would disobey and summing up in himself every human experience. On behalf of all victims, he absorbs all victimhood, and on behalf of the lonely, he becomes the definitive outcast upon the cross. He opens the way for entrance into God's place of secrecy: the Most Holy Place where the most intimate friendship can start to take shape. Here within the glow of his glory, outcasts the world over are sharing in the secrets of God. From this moment of abject godforsakenness flows intimacy of the richest kind.

Text: Matthew 27:46; Mark 15:34

Prayer: Lord Jesus, would you heal me of the things that have driven me to this lonely place, and remind me that I am not alone. And now Lord, welcome me, I pray, into the secret place of intimacy with you. Amen.

"I thirst"

Ever woken up in the night with that awareness that your whole mouth and gullet have completely dried out? It makes you cough and swallow. Your tongue feels like it doesn't belong to you. You go to the bathroom for a glass of water. There is a perfectly natural cause. You were perhaps a little dehydrated when you went to bed and then you slept with your mouth wide open, possibly because your nose was congested. Similarly here, with this doubtless very faint utterance only audable to those nearest the cross, we have a description of something physical and rather normal: "I thirst." The intense thirst has been brought on by the loss of blood and other fluids and the body has gone into shock. Death is very near. "I thirst" shows us that Jesus Christ was absolutely human with a body exactly like ours but beyond that I feel reluctant to read too much into the phrase. "I'm thirsty." Of course he is, so would I be: maddeningly.

The fifth saying from the cross is unique to John. John, it seems, took Jesus at his word and, in response to the third saying, left the scene of the cross as soon as Jesus gave the instruction about his mother. He quite literally removes her from the hill at that point and takes her to back to his house where she could eat and drink with others that were gathered there and be refreshed. This is how it is that John misses the fourth saying. Had he been an eye witness of words of such theological depth, he doubtless would have had something to say about them in his Gospel. Now he arrives back on the scene and has approached close enough to see what appears now to be a lifeless Jesus. Has his cousin passed away and he wasn't there with him? Then comes a low croaking sound and the mouth begins to part. Slowly, on broken lips, the words are formed: "I . . . thirst . . ." Surprisingly, John introduces this saying as being uttered, "so that the Scriptures might be fulfilled." What Scripture? Where? Probably John is here noticing that Jesus is fulfilling Psalm 69:21. This psalm speaks of being offered vinegar to drink. Accordingly, using a sponge and a long spear, the soldiers respond to Jesus' plea by offering him some of their own *posca* (a mixture of sour wine, water and beaten eggs, not to be confused with the drugged wine he had earlier refused), which he gladly takes. Matthew and Mark also record this event but offer no comment on it. An alternative view is that John understands Jesus to be quoting Psalm 42:2: "My soul thirsts for God, for the living God. Oh when can I come and appear before God?" Except that he only manages to quote the words "I thirst." On this view, the thirst would be spiritual, relating to how he feels deserted by God. The second view is better to preach on and write about but the first option seems to make far more sense to me, and seems to be followed by most scholars.

So where does this leave us? We are beholding a man at the very edge of death. He is staring it in the face and his body is about to shut down. Yet he is also claiming in some way to be representing all of us, claiming to be a "ransom for many" who is laying his life down for his sheep. "No one takes it from me," he had said. He claimed to have the power to lay it down and the power to take it up again. Yet here, seemingly, is somone in a most pathetic state, who is being consumed by the creeping symptoms of death, the feverish final moments of life violently brought to an end by cruel humanity. The one who once claimed to be the source of a living water that if someone were to drink, they would never thirst again, is now in need of a sip of the soldiers' sour wine.

This word only makes sense when it is intertwined with the sixth word. John ties the two together as an inseparable pair of sayings. This sixth word, as we will see, is a word of triumph. He is taking a drink in order to recover just enough physical strength to say it and to say it loud and clear.

Text: John 19:28.

"It is finished"

Until now, there had been only darkness, thick and impenetrable, and weakness almost to the point of losing consciousness. The pain had given way to numbness in all of his extremities. Now, the darkness has begun to lift and, following his small drink, some physical strength has started to return. There is now the giddy, painless lightheadedness that immediately precedes death. He raises himself up to proclaim one of the best known sayings from the cross: "It is finished." It leaves us with almost as many questions as the cry of dereliction. In this case our question naturally is: if this refers to something more that simply the completion of Jesus' own life and mission, if is of wider significance—and, in view of his own opinion of what his death was supposed to accomplish we may be sure that it does have a wider significance—then why, in the face of a finished act of redempion, do we still live in a world so choc-full of misery of every kind?

Well, let's try to understand "It is finished" from the viewpoint of the guy that wrote this, the only one of the four Gospel writers to include the phrase. John had a set of favourite words that he felt contained a whole world of truth. Words like: light, life, love, witness, truth, will, some of which were paired with opposites: darkness, death, hate and lies. Jesus is pictured as the one, serene and gracious, introducing these good things to a hostile world that keeps misunderstanding him. Not very prominent but still distinctive of John are the ideas of work and completion. "My food," said Jesus, "is to do the will of him who sent me and to finish his work" (John 4:34). He explains that he has come down from heaven to finish the work that his Father had given him to do and, just before going to the cross, says to the Father, "I have finished the work You have given me to do" (John 17:4). He talks a lot about working works, working while it is still day and the work of God. This work, it seems, had now reached its ultimate moment of completion.

In our own lives that sense of completion is so rare that we tend to remember our great finishing lines very clearly. These moments are a contrast with the norm of never going home with a clear desk, never having an empty inbox, never having an empty washing basket, never finishing a DIY project, or the warped painting in the shed without a sky, or that novel that started so well but fizzled out after a few pages. The moment I received an email from Bangor University saying, "Congratulations, you have passed your PhD," is a moment I will never forget. The impact on my sense of self esteem was impossible to predict. The next day I didn't walk into the call centre where I worked, I floated. It was a moment when, not only was a work done, a process completed, but an ongoing change was secured. My very title had now changed. Things would never be the same again.

So what was this work that the Father had given Jesus to do? What was it that had now reached its point of completion in these few precious moments on the cross before the great Prophet bowed his head and handed over his spirit? As far as John is concerned, the opposite of Jesus working and completing is humans believing and abiding. He makes a point of recalling the time that Jesus said, "This is the work of God, that you believe in him whom he sent" (John 6:29), and is the only Gospel writer to give us the benefit of a moment when Jesus, after his last meal with his apostles, sets off for the Mount of Olives waxing lyrical about vines and branches. "I am the vine," said Jesus, "You are the branches . . . he who abides in me bears much fruit" (John 15:1–5). He has done a work that it is not our part to join in with or add anything to. We can only trust and rest, abide and draw sap.

At this point we need to pan out wider still to the creation of the world itself. Whatever may be our theory about how or when the universe was made, the creation poem of the first book of the Bible wants us to know that it was a work of God. And that work of

God was followed, on what it describes as the seventh day, by rest. Adam, you may know, was created on the sixth day. So the very first full day of the first man's existence, was a day of rest, a sabbath. Ever since then, the Jewish day has begun with the feasting family time of the evening and a good night's sleep. It begins with rest and is followed by fruitfulness the following morning. The typical Jew would have been an early riser and been about his business with the rising of the sun, but this was not the start of the day. The day started the previous evening. This fact was brought out to the full each Friday when, at 6pm, all work would have to cease for 24 hours and even when Sabbath was over, there would be more feasting, family time and sleep.

John describes Jesus as the Word that created the universe, the one that spoke it into being. Now, with these final words, Jesus begins to speak a new creation into being. His work is done and his followers must trust the work and abide in it. Then, from that restful place fruit will come. When my mechanic has finished looking at my car and hands me the bill, it may well itemise each task but I am not well placed to assess whether such things needed doing or why. I have to trust—which can be hard when it comes to mechanics. Not so with Jesus. John does not greatly enlarge on what the great work it is that Christ has accomplished for us. It's just that, when with the eyes of our spirits we see him hanging there, the holy, harmless, mighty Son of God, we see our own completeness. We know that if we trust this Man that all manner of thing shall be well. All that you or I ever ought to have been, finds its fulfilment in him. All that you or I ever should have finished off is finished off in him. All that you and I ever need pay is paid in full in the mighty one, the great high priest. The final sacrifice has now sat down in everlasting glory.

Text: John 19:30

Application: Hebrews 10:11–22

Prayer: Father, on the basis of the complete and perfect work of your Son, I draw near in the full assurance of trusting in the God-Man sat down, the crucified one at rest, the curtain forever torn in two. I come close to You now to experience the fullness of joy that alone is to be had in Your presence. Thank you so much.

"Into your hands . . ."

To trust is the greatest thing a human can do—so long as the right thing is trusted. I still remember my one experience of flying with Aeroflot from Moscow to Krasnadar in 1992. At that time this airline had one of the worst safety records of any airline in the world. Inside, the plane was like the inside of a vandalised bus. Seats had been torn from their places and white clouds of exhaust fumes poured into the plane from the rear as the plane sat on the runway with all of us on wobbly seats waiting inside. The staff, however, were friendly enough. In fact, the flight was highly participatory. One of our team was even allowed to have a go at flying the plane: an old DC10 I think it was. We took a photo of him in the cockpit pretending to talk down the little microphone while holding the joy stick—or whatever that thing is called. I have no idea about piloting planes—and neither had he. Much united and fervant prayer went up that day.

Even when we are in the hands of one of the world's best airlines, there is always that moment of trust as we take off. I don't know about you but that slight sweaty-palms feeling never quite goes away no matter how many times I've taken off. Instinct still says, "This should not be happening. Humans don't fly. This plane weighs far too much to successfully float around in the sky." But trust we must. The Shepherd's Psalm, the world's favourite psalm, is all about this. "The Lord is my Shepherd," the writer says, "I shall not be in want . . . he leads me . . . I will fear no evil . . . Surely goodness and mercy shall follow me . . ." Trust shields us from being tempted by harmful ways of getting our needs met. We absolutely must be carried and borne up on the wings of God, or else bump along the ground hitting one temptation and obstacle after another and never finally winning. And here, in this seventh and last word from the cross, Jesus, in perfect peace, shows us what trust is: "Father, into your hands I commit my spirit."

This is the prayer that every pious Jew would pray before going to sleep at night. It is a quotation from psalm 31:5 but with the word "Father" added at the start, so that both the first and last words from the cross begin with this familiar term of address. It is clear that any sense that God had been at a distance is now gone and Jesus, in the language of family, expresses his complete trust in God the Father as he hands over his spirit.

Another thing to notice about this last saying is the phrase, "I commit," and the description following, "bowing his head he breathed his last." Similarly, we have John's phrase, "he handed over the spirit." It is interesting that none of the Gospel writers simply say, "he died." Each one is wanting to draw our attention to the unusualness of the death. The active voice is used. Jesus willed himself to die. He chose the moment at which to hand over his spirit. He went to death not as just another one of its myriad victims but as its conqueror, paving the way for each of us who have first followed him to that place of trusting in God. And trust we must.

Text: Luke 23:46; Matthew 27:50; Mark 15:37; John 19:30

Application: Hebrews 13:6; Romans 8:37–39

Prayer: Father, I sometimes fear what people, the devil, life or death might do to me, but here and now I choose to put my trust in you alone. Amen.

FOUR

The Ten Appearances

Most are in hiding in Bethany, some are at John's house in Jerusalem. Everyone is misreable and worried and tossing at night, grieving and traumatised at the same time, like soldiers regrouping after a bloody and terrifying defeat. Eyes are staring. Faces are drawn. Food is uninteresting. Danger is in the air. For Jesus, there has been a strange glimmer of a reversal. After all the humiliation of the trials and crucifixion, his body has been sealed in a rich man's tomb together with 33 kgs of spices—a burial fit for a king. His body has been saved from the ususal fate for crucifixion victims in this part of the world: a mass grave.

It's Sunday morning.

To Mary Magdelene

All the way from Bethany, where nine of the apostles were in hiding, she had walked, having set off while it was still dark. Joining with Mary the wife of Cleopas (probably the sister of Jesus' earthly father) and with Salome (mother to James and John), she reached the tomb at daybreak. Mary Magdalene, the only one in this little company not related to the man in the tomb, felt she owed everything. She had strayed from her family home to frequent the taverns of notorious Magdala when Jesus first met her. Unlike her sister, Martha, she was rash and impulsive, adventurous and fun loving. Yet she could never have predicted the deep darkness that would fill her soul. Then, along came this man. He reached out a hand and gone were years of deepening captivity to things that made her hate herself. She left her life in Magdala to return home to Bethany and live with her irritable bossy sister once again. Jesus used to stay there during the festivals. She would hang on his every word. His words were like the rain, his presence like the blazing sun, his love like the sweet nourishment of dates, his laughter infectious. And now he was gone, and as she arrived at the tomb she was met with the most terrible sight. Not only had the Romans taken away a life that meant everything to her, someone had opened the tomb and even taken his body. Who could be so merciless as to shatter her whole world twice over, to destroy her and then take away the one last privilege she had sought: to return to the body and complete the embalming process that had been interrupted by the onset of Sabbath on Friday night? She ran to John's house, tears streaming down her cheeks, to tell Peter and John this terrible news.

The other Mary and Salome, stood at the tomb speechless for a time. They were joined by Joanna and Suzanna from Herod's Palace who had brought, out of their wealth, an abundance of spices. Emboldened by their arrival, this Mary and Salome with Joanna and Suzanna close behind, crept towards the entrance of the tomb, penetrating the eeriness that burial places the world over seem to possess. As they stooped through the entrance a faint glow was detectable in the otherwise pitch darkness of the interior. Perhaps someone had left an oil lamp in there and had forgotten to put it out. The tomb had a number of alcoves at various stages of completion. These had been carved out of the rock and were being prepared for Joseph of Arimathea's aging relatives. The far alcove was not immediately visible from the entrance. This was where the body of Jesus lay and from where, as the four women drew closer, the light was emanating. Mary was in front. She suddenly stopped. The other three collided with each other behind. They all looked. Open-mouthed, and with hearts racing, they stared at two men in glowing white, one sat at the head end and the other where the feet of Jesus had been.

There then transpires a lot of running. Mary Magdalene soon finds Peter and John and they all start out for the tomb. Meanwhile, via a different route, the four women who saw the angels inside the tomb are stumbling breathless through rocky gardens on their way to John's house to report what they have seen. Peter and John then thoroughly inspect the physical remains, while Mary Magdalene sits staring into space outside the tomb. Inside the tomb, the angels seem not to be visible to Peter and John, but what they do see simply amazes them. They behold a cocoon of empty grave clothes and the cloth that was around the head that kept the mouth closed neatly folded up. The thing that struck them was the perfect orderliness of it all. Nothing had been ripped open. All seemed so undisturbed. The body of Jesus had not been taken and dragged anywhere. It had upped and left. John was completely awe-struck by this. It was, quite literally, a spine-tingling sight. They both ran back to John's house to inform those who were lodging there.

Mary Magdalene stayed at the tomb, ignored by Peter and John as they ran off. Dazed, she sat and stared at the tomb as the first beams of sunshine soaked the garden, enriching the hues of bright flowers. After so much running around and shouting, she needed a moment to collect her thoughts. Her emotions had always been stronger than her thoughts and it was these, in the end, that took over. To her, all was confusion except this one thing: he was gone. The person who meant more to her than the whole world was gone. More than that: there was now no earthly trace of him. All was loss, loss, loss: nothing but absence, nothing but grief. Her chief joy was gone without a trace. She began to cry again.

Despite the strong emotions, some modicum of rational enquiry drew her closer to the entrance of the tomb. She went inside. Sure enough, those two angels, now visible again, were still there.

"Dear woman, why are you weeping?" they say.

"They have taken away my Lord and I don't know where they have put him," is her tearful reply as she turns to leave the tomb, so dazed by grief that she hardly reacts to the fact that she has just been conversing with angels. She returns to the rock she was sitting on before and faces the tomb sobbing. From behind there is another voice: "Dear woman, why are you crying? Whom do you seek?" She turns and sees a man. Thinking him to be the gardener she asks him whether perhaps he had taken the body and put it somewhere and if so, could she please retrieve it.

There then follows one of the most moving moments in the Bible. It is rather like that moment in *The Railway Children* when the eldest daughter, Roberta, begins to discern the figure of her long lost father through the steam of the railway platform and says those famous words: "Daddy! My Daddy!" The language alone shows us how special the moment is that ushers in the very first post-resurrection encounter with Jesus Christ. Everywhere else in the passage, Mary's Greek name, "Maria," is used. Likewise, everywhere else in the New Testament, "Jesus" or "Lord" or "Rabbi" is used. Here alone, as the risen Jesus stands behind the grieving Mary Magdalene, the actual word is reproduced that would have parted from the man who until this moment was taken for a gardener. He uses the Hebrew form: "Miriam!" With the sound of that voice speaking her name, recognition awakes. She turns for the second time, not now for a mere glance but to fill her watery eyes with a sight she thought she would never again see: "Rabonni!" "My Teacher!"

She clings to his ankles not wanting to risk losing the world again.

Text: John 20:11–18

Application: John 10:4; Hebrew 4:7–8

Prayer: Lord, in the midst of my emptiness, awaken my heart to recognize your voice calling my name, and open my eyes to see you involving yourself in my life. Amen.

To Two Other Women

Within a short while on that first day of the rest of history, all seven of those people we have so far met are back at John's house. First to arrive back are Mary the wife of Cleopas and Salome, together with Suzanna and Joanna who are expected back at the Palace soon. They breathlessly tell Cleopas, Mary the mother of Jesus and some other relatives who were staying there for Passover of the rolled away stone, the missing body and their encounter with the angels. Next, Peter and John barge through the door panting and placing hands on knees as they get their breath back, like returning joggers. Streaks of sun are coming through the little windows behind them and catching the dust in the air. The dazed company in the house are soon listening to further reports from each of them. This time it is various repetitious stammerings about "clothes" and "folded up . . . it was neatly folded up!" Not long after this, also panting and sweaty-faced, in rushes Mary Magdalene. She is positively glowing, beaming. To stunned silence, she even speaks of actually meeting and conversing with Jesus himself. She keeps lapsing into expressions of how it had all made her feel: "I was overjoyed . . . so relieved . . . the burden has gone . . . just gone. It's all gone!"

No one has much of an idea of what to make of this or what to do about it. It seems clear, though, with three sets of reports all testifying to something very bizarre having happened at the tomb, someone must go to inform the rest of the apostles. It was high time they were given an update of recent events in any case. Bethany is the place to go to find the nine who are in hiding. Salome and Mary the wife Cleopas—we'll call her Auntie Mary—volunteer to go. They soon find themselves on that familiar road through the Kidron valley and up the other side to the Mount of Olives. As they ascend the hill and their conversation rests floods of memories come back of times they accompanied Jesus on this road and the things he had said. All of that had now come under review in light of these strange events yet their minds could not as yet arrive at a definite conclusion. Perhaps there was more. Maybe they too would have a personal encounter with Jesus just like Mary Magdalene. This would finally confirm everything. How they longed to be able to arrive at Bethany with something more definite than a set of confusing reports and angelic encounters.

A few pilgrims pass them on the road. The Feast of Unleavened Bread is beginning and many are still camped on the hillside. In fact, pilgrims from Galilee typically pitched their tents in this place. There are some familiar faces but Auntie Mary and Salome keep their faces hidden. Greetings were apt to be lengthy and they were on important business.

Soon, they have passed the "Galilee" campsite and are on a slowly descending plateau that will take them to Bethany within twenty minutes. Mount Nebo and the range of barren hills beyond Jordan that reach through historic Ammon and Moab fill the shimmering horizon. The sky is a vast and clear expanse. No one is around. Everywhere seems quite still. The atmosphere seems to have changed. An unbidden joy rises within and happy thoughts dispel all worry. It is like a little taste of heaven. They turn to look at one another. "Rejoice!" says a voice, laughing. They turn to face the gleeful Conqueror of death, and before they know what to say or do they find themselves at his feet in worship. Out of the clear blue sky his brown eyes look down: "Do not be afraid but go and tell my brothers to go before me into Galilee and there they will see me."

They had set out from Jerusalem with half a message. They would arrive at Bethany with the gospel.

Text: Matthew 28:9–10

Prayer: Lord, like the messengers on the road, may I also meet with you in such a way that I am full of good news to tell. Amen.

To the Two on the Road to Emmaus

Cleopas turns to Luke: "Are you ready?" and off they go. They set off from the Zebedee household into the dazzling brightness of the street that is now busy with people. Both are eager to get away from the crowds and process all of the strange reports they have been hearing. In common with the others, they have not had much sleep over recent nights and are irritable.

They leave Jerusalem by the West gate and proceed North along a good Roman road. They soon find themselves ascending a hill that leads to a plateau. The terrain is rocky and the Roman road gives way to a dirt track. The sun is at its height now and, even for Spring, it is getting hot. As soon as they recover from the climb, the debate starts. This, you understand, is a Middle Eastern debate. There are no subtleties; no double negatives, no offers of, "Well, it's not impossible that . . ." or, "Of course, perfectly credible though that may be, we have to bear in mind that . . ." which is the kind of conversation that would transpire had the resurrection happened in Surrey. This was more like the kind of contretemps one might encounter in a coffee shop in Spain. During a holiday there I quickly learned that aggression was the default posture of Spanish men, who might otherwise be the best of friends and may only be discussing the football results, and of a team they both support.

Soon, the two men find themselves at the bottom of a valley at the head of which is the pretty village of Emmaus, the "Place of Warm Springs" renowned as a place of healing where Luke the physician, to whose house they were heading, lived and worked. They are not one hour into their seven-mile journey and the landscape has changed dramatically. All around is verdant. Quaint villas nestle within flowery gardens with creepers overflowing the walls. Everywhere there are groves of oranges, lemons and olives. The road they travel has become beautiful. It is a perfect Spring day. Oblivious to this, the two men go on arguing. The Greek word that Luke himself uses in his Gospel to describe the conversation is, *antiballō*, a word that implies hurling things at one another, in this case words. They cannot agree on the true meaning of their murdered messiah's teachings. All is confusion.

Then, the atmosphere changes. The bickering goes on but a luxuriant peace now surrounds them like the enchanted glow that envelopes the cots of babies the world over as they sleep. The sunshine is now full of heavenly brightness. They both sense something that seems to be sucking the aggression out of their words. What would have been said with venom is said in a more hesitant way. Their ears are opened to one another and their hearts begin to feel each other's sorrows. There is a footfall behind them. They both stop talking but continue walking, listening as the sound of the feet unhurriedly draws closer. Something in their hearts says that this sound is a welcome thing. They turn to the stranger.

"Greetings!" says the stranger. "So what is this heated discussion you've been having?"

They spill their anxieties about the events of the last three days, about all that "we had hoped" and about the perplexing reports of the women. The curious stranger, who initially seemed so ignorant about recent events in Jerusalem, suddenly seems to know more than they do about it: "O this is silly. How could you be so slow to believe what the Scriptures teach?" he says, "Don't you understand how the prophets all along foretold that the Christ would first suffer before entering his glory?" The rest of the road up through the valley then consists of this very erudite stranger explaining from all the Scriptures the significance of all the predictions about the Messiah.

Finally, they reach a junction. The stranger seems to be planning to carry on down a different road. They constrain him: "Stay with us," says Luke, "The day is already far spent," and by this he meant that it was now the afternoon, not necessarily the evening.

They both hoped that the stranger would accept that he is better to stay with them for the night than try to get to wherever he is bound in what is left of the day. The stranger obliges. Luke's home is not opulent but a great place for practicing hospitality. There is a spacious dining area where the three men recline on couches. Leaning on their left elbows they allow servants to attend to washing feet, anointing hair and bringing out the aperitif of honeyed wine. Soon it is gone three o'clock in the afternoon as leisurely conversation continues. The main course arrives, which is served with bread. The stranger, whose company had been so immensely enjoyable, takes a loaf and looks up to heaven, saying, "Blessed are you, Lord our God, Ruler of the universe, who brings forth bread from the earth." He looks at the two disciples, a glint in his eye and starting to smile. Recognition is dawning across their faces. He looks at the bread in front of his face. Glowing a little, he breaks it. The broken bread falls upon the couch, one half tumbles on down to the floor. The welcome Stranger has vanished.

Text: Luke 24:13–35

Prayer: Risen Lord Jesus, I acknowledge that, like the arguing disciples, I have often been too overtaken with worry and strife to notice that you have drawn near to me. I welcome you into fellowship with me this moment and I pray that you would open my eyes to your wonderful presence in my life today. Amen.

To Peter

While all this was going on, in the middle of the afternoon, we find Peter outside the walls in a dusty deserted spot. He is in a fetal position with his head encased in his big burley hands. Tears and saliva are attracting dust that clings to his face. His eyes are screwed, each wrinkle tracing the many-faceted torment he had been feeling—and still feels. He is the one disciple who had made the biggest, most public and least forgivable blunder of the last three days: he denied he knew the person who meant the most to him. A servant girl had made him cave in and with increasing vehemence—with oaths and curses—he had, three times over denied Jesus in His hour of trial. At the very moment Jesus had owned up to who he was before Caiaphas, Peter was strenuously disentangling himself from all association, feigning a posh accent to conceal his Galilean northernness. And now it seemed his torment was being increased to an unbearable weight, for the one to whom he had once said, "Depart from me for I am a sinful man," was now beside him. The hand of the risen Jesus rested on his shoulder. Jesus had met him along the dusty path this very afternoon. He had tumbled to the ground and now, his diaphragm would hardly let in any air. It was like those times when he had been dreaming and was crying in the dream. Then he had woken up because his body needed to breathe. So now, there was almost no air going in. Jesus knelt on the ground alongside his guilt-stricken friend and whispered some words in his ear. We see Peter's back ceasing to pulsate and he is calm, sniffing. Soon, they both stand. A warm embrace seals Peter's forgiveness and he is so glad, so relieved. Who knows what the future could hold now. He can live.

Text: Luke 24:34; 1 Corinthians 15:5

Prayer: Risen Lord Jesus, I ask that I too may know your forgiveness for mistakes of mine that were just as deliberate, emphatic, and public as Peter's. In your mercy, release me from the shame I carry to live a full and glad life for you. Amen.

To the Ten

The nine at Bethany had judged appropriately the significance of recent reports and, in response to Salome and Mary's news, had made their way to Jerusalem to assemble with the others, this time in John Mark's house in the large upper room, the same upper room that had been the location for the last supper. It is evening, and a considerable meal is being prepared. They all make their way in hushed conversation up the steps on the side of the house to the roof and the guest room. Gathering with the nine are Peter and John, Cleopas and Luke, and the three Marys. Meanwhile, the empty tomb itself had become something of a local attraction, there being even at this moment a small gathering of curious people kept at bay by a division of Roman guards. The fear that all this attention might soon switch to them made them bolt the door. Being locked together in a room so full of vivid memories welded them together, though Thomas was not among them. The aroma of coriander and cumin drifted into the room as the little company of future world-changers reclined with their drinks. As first Mary Magdalene related her story, then Salome and Auntie Mary, then Cleopas and Luke theirs, then Peter his, a sense of expectation rose. Then, the food was brought, a delicious fish dish—fresh from Galilee, and everyone's minds soon shifted to their hungry stomachs. Hands reached for the unleavened bread.

Quite suddenly, a different kind of aroma filled the room: sweet, heavenly. Out of the corner of a number of diners' eyes, a figure appeared, standing. They turned and saw him. "Peace to you," he said. But hearts that had been relying on bolted doors for a sense of safety and seclusion were now deeply troubled. How could he have got in?

There was no mistaking who this was. Here was the same man that had eaten his very last meal with them in this room. Now, it seems he had come to share the first meal of his new life with them too. He asked for some fish to eat. This he explained was to demonstrate that he was real and physical, not a ghost or apparition. John dutifully passed him some fish and gazed at him in wonder and joy as Jesus took it and ate using all his usual mannerisms. As he finished the piece of fish, Jesus reiterated his reassurance that he had real flesh and bones and was not a ghost. He even still bore the wounds of his crucifixion, a fact that he seemed to be not in the least ashamed of and pointed to them a number of times, even pulling away clothing to show the spear wound in his side.

Here was the victim of terrible violence transfigured into the ultimate victor and in need of no revenge. He was the same yet different. He definitely seemed to glow a little and looked perhaps a few years younger and fresher than he did at the end of three years of very demanding ministry. To Peter he looked a lot better than he did that night when the cock crowed and they exchanged glances. To John he looked a lot happier than that lonely night among the ancient olive trees just before his arrest. He looked satisfied. This was no longer the man on a mission that they had tried so hard to keep up with. His was no longer the face set like flint. He looked and sounded like he wanted to laugh: as though some funny thought had just come to him and he was trying to hold it back. He continued like this as he stood chatting to them and answering questions, soon taking up a seat on one of the couches. He was in full voice, explaining with great anticipation about how he was sending them into the world in just the same way that the Father had sent him. He did not recline for food and the food of all his listeners soon went cold as they hung on his every word, motionless. They all began to feel so very comforted. Then, he surprised them all again. He stopped. He opened his mouth and, without having taken in any air, started breathing out. The remarkable thing was the effect of his blowing on them. The whole room was filled with a strong breeze. One of the servants felt it and needed to sit down. "Receive the Holy Spirit," he said, and sure enough, something like waves of joy, liquid love, began to pass through every person in the room. They each felt themselves being filled with a deeply reassuring presence. The Great Forgiver then reminded them of one of his teachings with which they were so familiar: the importance of forgiving others. Immediately there sprang to everyone's mind all those that had contributed to the pain of the last few days: the religious establishment, the hated Romans. Then he vanished.

Text: John 20:19–23

Application: Genesis 2:7; 1 Corinthians 15:45

Prayer: Risen Lord Jesus, you are welcome in my home. Please come and dine with me and those closest to me. Make your presence felt among us. Breathe into us the Holy Spirit to recreate us and make us new on the inside. Amen.

To the Eleven

Five of the ten appearances all happened in the first day. He appeared first to a woman with a shady past, then to some more women, then to a faithful follower that had fallen, then to two arguing men that weren't even apostles. Last of all, he had appeared to the apostles. There was, of course, one apostle that was absent, the one we commonly call "Doubting Thomas."

It is clear that he was not disloyal but was someone who needed to "get his head around things" first. He may well not have doubted at all the reports he had heard but, rather, understood how momentous these facts were if they were actually true. If it was actually true that Jesus was now the first person ever to have stared death down, got his life back, won his body back from the grave and now, seemingly, was appearing and disappearing at will and was on his way "back to the Father," then truly a new age had just dawned. If this was the first installment of the great "Day of the Lord," when all wrongs would be righted and God's life begin to course anew through all creation, then he wanted in. But because he had thought so long and hard about these things, he wanted to be sure. Like a modern scientist just about of announce some new medical breakthrough to the world, he wanted to test his findings as thoroughly as possible. He wanted to eliminate all risk of having been mistaken, of having believed in phantom appearances and visions.

The test he desired was very thorough: "Unless I see in his hands the place of the nails and put my finger into the place of the nails, and put my hand into his side, I will not believe." After all the excitement, one could be forgiven for finding Thomas' no-nonsense approach quite refreshing. It served him well too. Not only do we owe to him the arrival of Christianity to South India where it thrives to this day, but here, on this night, a week after the first Easter Sunday as the disciples are again gathered to eat, the Lord honors this man's request. Again the doors are locked. Again, Jesus appears. Again, he says, "Peace to you." Then Jesus, turning to his most loyal skeptic, invites him with a smile to come and carry out the very test he had said to the others in such strident tones that he wanted to carry out. Thomas is open-mouthed. In the end, it seems, there is no need. He falls down and says, "My Lord and my God." Jesus, on this eighth day after Easter, then utters the ninth Beatitude: "Blessed are those who have not seen and yet have believed."

Ask him to make himself known in a tangible way: an actual hand on the shoulder, actual words spoken into your ears, real feelings rising within your heart, dark clouds of discouragement really lifting, anxieties taking wings and flying away.

Text: John 20:24–29

Application: Ephesians 1:15–23; Romans 10:9

Prayer: Risen Lord Jesus, reach into my life today in a way that reminds me that you are real, on the move and ready to love. Lord, help me to believe and keep on believing; to trust and to keep on trusting in you. Amen.

Beside the Lake

The Feast of Unleavened Bread now over, the Eleven headed back to Galilee to their various trades there. Jesus had promised that he would go ahead of them and meet them there. Even after such dramatic encounters, it seems expectations were not very high. With the return to familiar homes, familiar streets, and groves and gardens that had changed only in the flowers that had opened while they had been away, familiar unbelief also returned. The events of the last few days seemed like a dream. They would be going about their business and then remember him sitting down with them in the Upper Room as they ate fish. Then, the memory would pass as soon as it had come. A lot of memories were doing this in a lot of their minds—especially Thomas.' After all, there was not only the resurrection but three years of the most amazing miracles on these very shores all requiring to be processed and filed away in some place that made sense. Peter still would sometimes lie awake all night, his young mind trying to process everything: the feeding of the five thousand, the electrifying sermons in the synagogues, the young lad being raised from the dead at his funeral, and now, the empty tomb, the sudden appearances and disappearances and explanations from the Scriptures, the breathing out of the Holy Spirit. There was still a sense that they were part of an as yet unfinished story.

"I'm going fishing," said Peter after they had finished the evening meal. The evening was exceptionally mild and his fishing instincts told him the conditions were good for a night trawl. Six others joined him in the boat, all with some excitement. By 11.30pm, they had all lost count of the number of times they had hauled up an empty net and the yawning began to spread. By 1am, the desire for sleep had past but all their arms were aching from constant handling of the heavy net and their hands were throbbing. They kept going. Peter was determined, impetuous. 5am, and the first glow of light began to appear and a mist lay over the water. The dawn soon took on a rosier, warmer complexion and lovely streaks of orange adorned the horizon. Their tummies rumbled. Activity ceased. The Lake was very still.

A figure stood on the shore. John stared at this figure. It turned and walked along the beach and then stood again and seemed to look straight at him. "Boys!" the figure said, "Have you caught any food?" His voice carried well as it bounced off the water and through the chilly air.

"No!"

"Then cast you net on the right side of the boat and you will find some!" Exhausted and stiff, they all rose to their feet and let the net down one more time. Within moments they felt that profoundly reassuring resistance, that heavy drag on the boat, which told fisherman all over this Lake: "yes, you will feed your family again tonight, all is well." However, this pull was far stronger than normal. In fact, all seven of them were completely unable to bring up the net. John pulled himself away from the tussle of men's arms and flapping fish and took another look at the man standing on the shore who now had his hands on his hips smiling proudly. Blood drained from his cheeks as the realization came, just as shocking as in Jerusalem. He turned to Peter: "It . . . it's the Lord!" Soon there would be breakfast on the beach.

Text: John 21:1–14

Prayer: Lord, I have toiled and caught nothing, I have tried and tried and still not succeeded, I have labored and go unrewarded, I need a miracle. Lord, you are the same as on that beautiful morning by the sea. Be my miracle this week. Amen.

To Five Hundred at Once

However optimistic Jesus was about investing all of himself in a tiny handful of people who would be empowered to change the world, he was also realistic enough to know that a much bigger gesture was needed. So, after breakfast on the beach, he gave the seven who were present details of a hill in Galilee where, not only the Eleven and other hangers-on would gather, but as many as possible of the people that had followed him from town to town throughout his three years of Galilean ministry were to be invited.

This task soon took on the form of a covert operation as the apostles gathered and talked through the night by lamp light compiling list after list of names—anyone they could remember. There was a list for every village. Then, messengers were sent to each village who, after a brief glance over the shoulder to watch for any of Herod's henchmen, would rap on a door or whisper through a window. This meeting was by invitation only. With so much controversy surrounding the figure of Jesus Christ, discretion was of the essence.

When the day came, no one was sure how many would turn up. Some had believed the rumors of a resurrection; some doubted. On a grassy hill overlooking the Lake as the sun rose, some five hundred people gathered—enough to get this new idea called the "Church" off to a survivable start. Bang on time but not in a hurry, Jesus came up the hillside as the crowd parted for him. The apostles all prostrated themselves. He stood right in the middle, turning as he spoke. He spoke of the message they were to preach: "repentance and the forgiveness of sins." He spoke of the power they would receive: how the "Holy Spirit" would "clothe" them.

This new power would come, not in Galilee but in the Holy City after they had once more made pilgrimage, this time for the upcoming feast of Pentecost, the third and last in the annual cycle. For the apostles and the others that had experienced the very first post-resurrection encounters, this meeting had a slightly alarming finality about it. It felt as if they were all about to be thrown out of their nest and made to fly. It had the feel of a battle brief. They are hanging on to every word, not from joy or delight but fear and trepidation, like listening to a sky-diving instructor just prior to your first ever leap from a plane. They knew they did not have the power or the courage to do any of the things he was commissioning them to do. Jesus, unperturbed, finished with these words:

"All power in heaven and earth has been given to me. Go, therefore, and make disciples of all nations, baptizing them in the name of the Father, the Son and the Holy Spirit, and teaching them to observe all things that I commanded you. And, lo, I am with you always, even to the end of the age."

Somehow, he then slipped away through the crowd and disappeared. The most comforting thought now, just as on each of the other occasions, was the certainty that this was still an unfinished story. As with his parables, the great story-teller himself would surely make a good job of drawing the threads of these little episodes together in a way that would inspire and empower them, though his endings were often surprising. For now, all they needed to do was keep following his instructions.

Text: 1 Corinthians 15:6; Matthew 28:16–20

Prayer: Lord, you have commissioned me to go and make a difference in the world yet I know that I lack the courage and the power. But I agree to keep following your instructions as you take me, step-by-step, into your amazing destiny for me. Amen.

To James

The book of James in the New Testament has no fewer than 26 parallels with the Sermon on the Mount. It is full of borrowed sayings of Jesus (the most obvious being James 5:12 and Matt 5:34–37). The man who wrote this letter was quite obviously enamoured with the teachings of Jesus. Like Jesus, James speaks in pictures from everyday life: waves of the sea, withered flowers, mirrors, bits in horses' mouths, rudders of ships, forest fires, taming animals, springs of water, moth-eaten clothes and patient farmers.

Who could have written such a work? None other than James the brother of Jesus. Jesus had four brothers: James, Joses, Simon and Jude. In the Gospels we find the Lord's brothers to be cynical and unbelieving throughout the years of his ministry. Yet by the time we get to Acts 1:14, a dramatic change has taken place. There we find them gathered for prayer in Jerusalem at Pentecost along with their mother and the other 115 disciples who were all prayerfully waiting for God's power. We do not know what must have happened to Joses, Simon and Jude to account for this change but we do know what must have happened to James. It is recorded in 1 Corinthians 15:7 that this man actually had an encounter with the risen Lord. He was converted through seeing his own brother risen from the dead.

We can perhaps imagine the pain of one that has not paid attention when he had the chance. All he did was mock the ministry of his brother while it was going on and was rarely present to hear His teaching. Now all he can do is ask Peter, "What was it like when He did that?" and "What happened when He said that?" and

"So what did He say to that?" He must have felt humbled by knowing whose brother he was and zealous to propagate the teaching he had once ignored.

This zeal made James become the leader of the church at Jerusalem alongside Peter where he became a great champion of the poor. He won a reputation for righteous living in the early church, acquiring the nickname of James the Just. James was very popular, not only among Jewish Christians but non-Christian Jews as well, chiefly because of his concern for the poor of Jerusalem. The poor lived in cramped streets down-wind of the sewers while the rich resided in Upper Jerusalem. Many rural Jews had become landless and were being forced to pay heavy taxes of produce to oppressive landlords. James was outspoken about this and insisted that his churches must always open their hearts to the poor and not give preferencial treatment to the rich. Such was James' popularity with the common people that when the High Priest Annas II had him stoned to death in AD62, there was a public outcry. The outcry became so great that Annas was forced to surrender his office.

Sadly, as with Peter's private encounter, we know nothing of the event itself when the cynical brother that was closest to Jesus in age is suddenly turned from cynic to zealous believer. But what do we take from this? That God can. God can and does meet with the most inoculated—in this case by sheer familiarity. In other cases, the trappings of religion itself might be the barrier, but a personal encounter is possible. And people who have such private audiences with the King have a way of going on to become very significant people.

Text: 1 Corinthians 15:7; John 7:1–5; Mark 3:21; Gal 1:18–19

Application: Risen Christ, make yourself known personally and privately to those whom I know that are the most resistent to you, and may they become a significant blessing to the world. Amen.

Ascension Day

It is now ten days before Pentecost. Forty days have now elapsed in which Jesus has been gradually weaning his followers off the need for his continual physical presence and getting them used to the fact that he really had physically been raised from the dead in a renewed body and that these weren't ghostly or apparitional appearances. They were no longer spooked when he appeared. They felt sure that one day they too would share in his resurrection. He had also begun to teach them more and more about their coming mission to the world and the empowerment of the Spirit that would thrust them into it.

Once again, discretion was needed, especially now that they were back in Jerusalem having arrived early for the feast. Before dawn, Jesus, by prior arrangement, met with only the Eleven in the upper room at John Mark's house before leading them all by that familiar route across the Kidron Valley and up the other side to the Mount of Olives, chatting all the while with John, James, Matthias, Peter, James the Less, Thomas. Despite the undisguised closeness to him of Peter, James and John, Jesus had a way of making everyone feel special. Often just a glance was enough, but it was such a knowing and interested look, that one immediately felt important. It was a tailored look too, not standard for everyone. His eyes penetrated in a way that terrified the demonized but reassured the faithful.

They came as far as the place at the top of the Mount where the road begins its descent into Bethany. They had been talking much about the kingdom and it was evident that the souls of these boys were now fully restored to the old fervor and expectation.

The first words he says when there is a pause at the summit are in answer to one of the old-style fervent questions: "Are you at this time going to restore the kingdom to Israel?" He warns them not to worry about the time when this would happen. He promises them instead a more immediate result: "But you will receive power when the Holy Spirit has come upon you and you will be my witnesses . . ." He tells them to wait until they are clothed with that power.

A mist was gathering, which was common for this time of year. Jesus began to glow a little. They all felt a flutter in their hearts, a kind of joy. His arms were lifted. "Farewell," he said, and a cloud enveloped him.

Text: Luke 24:44–52; Acts 1:1–14; 13:31

Prayer: Ascended Christ, send me now the promise of the Father, the Holy Spirit, and clothe me now with new power to bear witness to who you are. Amen.

Select Bibliography

Bishop, Jim, *The Day Christ Died*. London: Hodder & Stoughton, 1957.

Edersheim, Alfred, *The Life and Times of Jesus the Messiah*. Grand Rapids: Eerdmans, 1971.

Farrar, Frederic, *The Life of Christ*. London: Cassell, 1909.

Francisco, Don, "Come and Follow Me," *He's Alive*. Airlift Records, 1998.

Grieve, Val, *The Trial of Jesus*. Bromley: STL, 1990.

Hill, William, B., *The Life of Christ*. London: Revell, 1917.

Packer, James, I., "What Did the Cross Achieve?" *Tyndale Bulletin* 25 (1974), 25.

Pollock, John, *Jesus the Master*. Eastbourne: Kingsway, 1984.

Thomas, Gordon, *The Jesus Conspiracy*. Oxford: Lion, 1987.

Turner, Janice, "A Casting Couch Only Works in a Locked Room," *The Times* (March 2, 2013), 25.

Wenham, John, *Easter Enigma*. Carlisle: Paternoster, 1996.

Whittell, Giles, "Prisoner 590, Guantanamo Bay," *The Times Magazine* (March 16, 2013), 26–32.